CAREER
Secret
Sauce

Winning Strategies
for Building a Great Career

9

Dave Horne

Holtkamp and Leger Publishing ❧ Lewes, Delaware, U.S.A.

This book is written with the understanding that the author was not engaged in rendering legal services. The information included has been carefully prepared and is correct to the best of his knowledge as of the publication date. If you require legal or expert advice, the services of professionals should be used. The author disclaims any personal liability, either directly or indirectly, for advice or information presented in this book.

The information as described herein has been used successfully to obtain profitable business for some of the persons who have used it. Although all efforts have been expended to supply the latest in complete, accurate and up-to-date information, it must be understood that the ultimate success of the user is dependent upon market conditions, efforts expended by the user, and other variable factors that are beyond the control of the authors, and that neither the users' actual expenses nor profits are guaranteed nor implied.

Throughout this book, trademarked names are used. Rather than put a trademark symbol after every occurrence of the trademarked name, we used the names in an editorial fashion only, and to the benefit of the trademark owner, with no intention of infringement of the trademark.

At the time this edition was printed and released, all of the sites listed herein were active and accessible to anyone having access to the Internet. Neither the author nor the publisher is responsible for broken links, abandoned sites, or changes that are beyond their control.

Holtkamp and Leger Publishing
Lewes, Delaware, U.S.A.

978-0-9817998-0-3

Library of Congress Control Number: 2008930514

Dedications and Acknowledgements

This book is dedicated to my original career counselor, my late father Clyde James Horne. There is simply no way that I would have ever enjoyed this career without his constant guidance.

I would also like to acknowledge the following key people for their contributions to this book:

Bob Collings: For his incredible leadership and enabling me to work for such a great company straight out of college.

Jim Meagher: For the countless opportunities he brought my way and the work experience that became the basic grist behind Career Secret Sauce.

Kathy Cote: For her hand in helping me focus when I needed it most and demonstrating the career power of simply "doing what you say you'll do."

Romesh Wadhwani: For teaching me true leadership through his stellar example and providing me with an opportunity of a lifetime.

Natalie Horne: For her guiding hand in finding the right "voice" for my writing, exhaustive editing, and demonstrating first hand just how well Career Secret Sauce works by building such a great young career for herself. I'm very proud of you.

Finally, my darling wife, Susan, for supporting my career change from CEO to author and enabling me to be the man I am today.

Praise for Career Secret Sauce

"The strategies offered in Career Secret Sauce provide many useful tools and real life examples of securing and creating a successful career. There is something for everyone, whether just embarking on their first career or looking to enhance their current career opportunities."

Thomas M. Tippett
Vice President-HR (Retired)
Allstate Insurance Company

"Dave Horne discovered that most people's natural instincts about how to get promoted are not only flawed, but can actually be self-destructive. His science of Promotionology really hits the nail on the head."

Jay Ennesser
Vice President
IBM

"Dave Horne has a way of explaining career success to today's generation that really connects. He recognizes that a flavorful career requires just the right blend of ingredients and seasoning from the very beginning, and he provides a relevant recipe."

Valerie Terry, Ph.D.
Pepperdine University

"Dave Horne has captured the essential building blocks for a great career!"

Penelope Trunk, Author
Brazen Careerist: The New Rules for Success

"Career Secret Sauce is an important resource for people who want a successful career and (here is the secret) are not willing to sacrifice their personal life to get it."

Dr. Paul Powers, Author
Winning Job Interviews and Love Your Job

Table of Contents

INTRODUCTION

Don't Take Your First Career Step On The Wrong Foot

Our job and career are vital to the quality of our lives. In many ways they define who we are, put food on our table, enable our families to live in nice homes, and hopefully pay for our kids to get a good education. They consume the majority of our waking hours. We go to school for 16 years or more to prepare for work and if anything goes sour, we lay awake at night worrying about it. It's tough stuff, but as Sinatra said, "that's life."

According to research from the Employment Policy Foundation, 46 percent of new hires don't last 18 months on the job. Getting fired is devastating at any time on your career, but being fired from your first job can damage your career beyond repair. The truth is that new workers are almost never fired for "not knowing their stuff." Recent college graduates usually know more about their profession than their superiors who have been out of school for 10 years. People who get fired from their first job generally do so by making classic rookie mistakes:

1. Too Academic—Wide-eyed recent college graduates often fail to appreciate that much of the "art and science" they learned in school is highly impractical in the business world. In their zeal to apply what they learned in school, they inadvertently demean the

1

intelligence of their coworkers. Or, they come off as perfectionist, inflexible dreamers.

2. Political Cannon Fodder—More savvy graduates believe that the business world is the opposite of academia. Blindly following the old saying "it's not what you know, but who you know," they see everyone they meet through political lenses. They align themselves with people they perceive as having power and disregard the little people. The enemies you make in school seldom come back to haunt you. They graduate, change majors and seem to eventually disappear. This is not the case in the white-collar workplace where people stay in one position for years and hold grudges for even longer. Get caught in a political skirmish before your time and you'll quickly become the scapegoat.

3. Animal House—Right or wrong, people start to size you up as soon as you walk through the door. Work hours, deadlines, and lifestyle factors have huge significance in the real world. College was a lot of fun, but for your boss and most of the influential people in your new job, it was a long time ago and nothing more than a semi-vacation. If you want to be taken seriously, forget your college days and immediately immerse yourself into the next chapter of your life: your new career.

Surviving the first few months of your career won't necessarily assure success; it will just keep you alive long enough to have a chance at excellence. Once you get your footing, you still need to create the right reputation, impress people around you, get promoted, and ultimately become a great leader. You can waste 10 years figuring everything out through trial and error like I did, or you can make it your business to learn these 9 winning strategies as soon as you can. I trust you'll choose the latter.

I wrote *Career Secret Sauce* to share what I have learned about creating a great career and still having a fulfilling personal life. I wrote it for people who have already decided on a career path and are looking for ways to increase their odds of success. The strategies in *Career Secret Sauce* are what I wish my professors had taught me in school. Whether you're just finishing college or well along in your career, these strategies can have a profound, beneficial, and immediate impact on your life and your livelihood.

The Three Phases Of Career Secret Sauce

Like any great human endeavor, you must crawl before you walk, and walk before you run.

In the case of your career this means:

Phase One—Get a clean start

Phase Two—Create a reputation as a future winner

Phase Three—Effectively navigate raises, promotions, and job changes

For some people in certain industries, it may take a decade to encounter all three of these phases. On the other hand, if you work in a volatile environment, you may find yourself facing these challenges during your first few years on the job.

Get A Clean Start

While the first few months on the job are critical, your chances of success actually began well before that. Hopefully, when you chose your career, you selected a profession you like and something you can be good at. But just because you picked the right field doesn't guarantee success or happiness with every employer in your elected vocation. You must pick an employer who suits you personally, get your first job, and make sure you play the game correctly during the ever-so-critical first 30 days on your new job.

Strategy 1: An Internship—Your First Big Career Break

Unless you have top grades from a top university, most companies won't hire you without experience. It's a classic Catch-22—you need experience to get a job, but the only way to get experience is from having a job! Fortunately, there is a solution: college internships. They're a lot easier to get than a real job and once you've landed your first internship, the second, third and fourth are a breeze. Strategy One discusses the benefits of an internship and how to go about getting one.

Strategy 2: Select An Employer That Suits Your Nature

Career success doesn't end with choosing the right vocation. The industry you select, the company you work for, and the geographic region you live in will set your career along a certain trajectory. The question is, is it the right trajectory for you? Or if you've already started working, is the trajectory your career is currently on helping or hurting your career? Strategy Two provides a framework for evaluating whether or not where you currently work suits your nature. It discusses the pros and cons of different venues and company characteristics.

Strategy 3: Thrive On Your New Job

Perhaps the most dramatic day in your life is the first day at the first serious job in your chosen career. Every bone in your body wants to start building a great career, but you're completely clueless about what to do. The questions you ask, the people you trust, the work you take on, and results you deliver will determine your future. This chapter provides practical advice for performing above expectations on your first job and setting the stage for long-term career growth.

Create A Reputation As A Future Winner

Simply avoiding crashing and burning during the first three to six months on the job doesn't guarantee career success; it just gets you into the game. From there, you have to build a solid reputation with the key people in the company. You can try to do everything right, but that's a lot of work and not much fun. I offer three proven strategies to help you establish a reputation as a future leader and set your career on a winning trajectory.

Strategy 4: Craft A Winning Reputation

It may not be obvious at first, but managers constantly keep score on everyone's behavior and coworkers love to gossip about each other's work habits. Unfortunately, this is often how the pecking order in the organization is scored. It would be great if your score was based on the merits of your work, but the sad truth is that your perceived work habits carry more weight than your actual work product. Once you know this, you can apply a little secret sauce to take control of the perceptions about your work habits and systematically create the reputation you need for a prosperous career.

Strategy 5: Do What You Say You'll Do

One of the biggest secrets to career success is so blatantly simple that people often miss it:—"just do what you say you're going to." The fifth strategy in *Career Secret Sauce* is a technique I call "The List" It transcends time management systems and provides a framework for actively determining the best use of your time on a daily basis. It is also a vehicle for turning the tables on office politics by proactively managing suggestions from every constituency at work to neutralize adversaries and convert them into allies. It provides a method for a systematic dialog with your boss, subordinates, coworkers, and other key executives for setting priorities and continuously demonstrating your invaluable contributions. This dialog not only assures you of solid job security, it also gives you a head start on your next promotion.

Strategy 6: Master The Art Of Presentation

The fear of public speaking has been widely publicized. Perhaps the most extreme finding was the 1973 Times of London survey of 3000 Americans that reported that 41 percent of those surveyed reported Fear of Public Speaking as their number one fear. Yes, public speaking can be scary at first, but therein lies the opportunity for the most powerful ingredient of Career Secret Sauce. Public speaking is not only scary for you, it's more than likely scary for your coworkers and even your boss. Unlike every other opportunity for glory on the job, most people don't volunteer for a speaking assignment. Once you learn how to speak well, you will harness the power to persuade and impress large groups of people with ease. The skill of public speaking is not that tough to conquer, but the fear of confronting an audience is so paralyzing that most people never even attempt it. The sixth strategy of *Career Secret Sauce* makes a compelling case for mastering public speaking, and then provides a series of simple techniques for learning how to do so.

Effectively Navigate Raises, Promotions, And Job Changes

Once you get on the radar screen with the right people, your success will come much quicker. If you've made the right moves, new opportunities will open up both inside the company and beyond. You can nurture these opportunities and strategically move ahead, or just go along for the ride. From time to time your career may run into trouble and you have to know how to quickly turn things around before any permanent damage occurs.

Strategy 7: Promotionology And The Art Of The Raise

Strong managers seldom volunteer raises and promotions. They want to see you work for them and retain these precious rewards as long as possible. Setting salaries and determining raises or bonuses is one of the last black arts in the industrial world. The seventh strategy details strategies for winning both incremental raises and major promotions. It also provides a background on the basics of compensation planning and administration.

Strategy 8: Career Saving Moves

Suddenly one day you wake up and realize that your job is at risk. Maybe you did everything right and the company or the economy just hit a speed bump. More likely, though, you inadvertently stepped into one of the dangerous career land mines described in this book and now you need to hustle to get back on the right track—or worse yet, to simply save your job. Strategy Eight covers a number of strategic moves that you can make to minimize the risk of this constant threat and techniques to save your career if the grim reaper strikes home.

Strategy 9: In Search Of Greener Pastures

There are very few companies that offer enough opportunity to fulfill a career. Those that do are usually huge, complex organizations that hinder personal individuality. This means a good career must include a number of strategic job changes. There is no magic number, but it's safe to say it's probably more than three and less than nine. Changing jobs can be one of the most stressful things you do to yourself, so you have to get it right. This chapter examines the mental side of changing jobs and outlines techniques to help you do it well. It also discusses the critical role of the search firm and how to create a win-win relationship that will serve your entire career.

The nine strategies in *Career Secret Sauce* will provide you with a solid platform for a great career. All you need to do is to learn them, apply them, and enjoy the life they bring.

PHASE ONE

Get a Clean Start

CAREER
Secret Sauce

STRATEGY ONE

An Internship—Your First Big Career Break

Winning your first job in your chosen vocation is a significant success. More than likely, however, it will also be the most difficult undertaking in your career. After graduation I spent 6 months looking for a job as an "apprentice architect" position before admitting that it probably didn't exist, and if it did, they were unlikely to ever hire me. After abandoning that dream, I started looking for any entry-level white-collar job that required a college degree and paid a decent wage. Since I was still living in my parent's basement and my father had connections with local executives, I had some help getting an interview with Data Terminal Systems (DTS). That opening ultimately led to my first job as Production Control Clerk. It was not what I dreamt of doing right out of college, and it paid only $3.25/hour (just barely more than minimum wage), but at least it was a start. Before the interview, I learned that DTS was a small, fast-growing, high-tech company and that many of the managers didn't even have college degrees. They were growing so fast, that they were outstripping the organizations ability to keep up. I went into the interview knowing that I would have ample opportunity for advancement and salary growth if I could get my foot in the door. For me, getting my first job meant swallowing my pride and taking what I could find. After 16 years of education I was happy to be a clerk.

11

Avoid Being A Painful New Hire

Outsourcing, immigration, and the growing trend of older workers postponing retirement means that it may be more difficult for you to land your first job in your chosen vocation than it was for me. That is, it will be if you do what I did and wait until you graduate to start thinking about how you're going to find your first job. If you take that route and walk into a prospective employer's office looking for a full time job without any relevant experience, you're likely to be turned down immediately. Unless you have a relative who's already a high-ranking employee, your chances of success are bleak. Without relevant experience, you're asking a hiring manager to make a bet on you; a wager with painful downside risk for him. For one thing, if you fail, people will question his judgment in hiring someone who obviously lacks experience. No one wants that kind of grief. On top of that, you're asking for a college graduate's full time salary and benefits, which isn't exactly chump change. Most importantly, you're asking the hiring manager to bet his or her reputation on your success. A "Bad Hire" (an employee who fails and must be fired) is one of the worst mistakes a manager can make. The people above him start questioning his managerial abilities and his subordinates lose respect. Hiring managers will go to great lengths to avoid a bad hire. That's why a college graduate with even a little experience will almost always be chosen ahead of someone who has none. The downside risk of a failed hire is just too painful.

Internships Are Virtually Risk Free For The Hiring Manager

By the same token, internships are attractive for a variety of reasons. First, you never have to fire an intern. Internships run for a fixed period of time, often as little as 8 weeks and when it's over, the intern just disappears. There's very little downside to hiring a dud. Second, intern programs are usually justified as a goodwill gesture to the community and local colleges, not critical resource decisions. Senior executives consider the hiring managers who take on internships as performing a company service rather than consuming additional personnel. Third, interns cost next to nothing, or perhaps even nothing. Most internships pay the prevailing minimum wage, or in the case of a coveted employer, they may not pay at all. Again, how much damage can a bad intern hire do if they're gone in 8 weeks and don't cost the company a dime? Unfortunately, therein lies the problem for you—the potential intern. The hiring manager may just be bringing you in to demonstrate good corporate citizenship and have nothing significant for you to do. If this happens, you'll find yourself facing 100+ hours of pure boredom and worse, you'll do very little to help your career. Securing college internships can give your career a huge boost out of the gate, but it can also turn into a waste of time if not done correctly. That's why "An Internship— Your First Big Career Break" is the first strategy in Career Secret Sauce.

It's Not An Internship; It's A Portfolio Of Experience

I have been talking about a college internship in the singular tense, but you should be thinking about creating a portfolio of internships between the first semester of your junior year and the last semester of your senior year— including the summer in between. For one thing, it will give you 4 or 5 experience highlights on your résumé rather than just one. You'll have more potential post-graduate job opportunities, more references, and undoubtedly learn more with each new assignment. Most importantly, if you pick assignments with different types of jobs in different size companies, you'll learn more about the kind of environment you'll flourish in.

Finding Your First Internship

I had never heard of internships when I was going to school, although the idea did occur to me in 1970. In order to improve my odds at landing that elusive apprentice architect position I was dreaming of, I persuaded a friend of mine to hire me for the summer as his designer. He owned a log cabin company and was having a tough time documenting exactly what it was that his customers were actually buying. While I did design a few homes, it did

13

nothing to help me get a real job after school. That's when I first learned all internships are not the same.

When considering an internship, you want to look for the following characteristics:

1. A place that is likely to offer you a job after graduation.

2. A location where you'd like to live.

3. A high quality company with a good reputation.

4. A decent supervisor who will let you do real work.

5. An assignment that complements, not duplicates, other internships.

Obviously my log cabin design job lacked most of these attributes. Once you have developed your own personal screen for evaluating potential employers, you need to drum up offers. The first place to check is your college or university. In many cases, it will have a listing of local companies who are hiring interns. If this works for you, it's all you need. But suppose your school doesn't offer this service, or there are no opportunities that fit your criteria—do you give up? Of course not! You just have to get creative. Your parents may be able to network among their colleagues and turn up something, or you can do the dirty work and start cold calling local companies.

My daughter Natalie had struck out getting an internship at a high profile public relations firm in Santa Monica, California during the fall of her junior year. A few weeks later, her marketing professor gave her class the assignment of taking a local executive out to lunch and learning about them. Natalie cold called the PR firm she was interested in and discovered that they had just hired a new CEO. She invited her to lunch, the new CEO accepted, and even insisted on paying! They had a great lunch at a posh sushi restaurant on Santa Monica Boulevard and at the end the CEO asked her to consider being an intern at her company. The next semester she followed up with the CEO and landed an internship with the company. She liked the idea of cold calling CEO's so much that she used the same technique on a food marketing company executive, receiving another offer for an internship that she took in her senior year. She is now working there as a part time employee and will likely be asked to become permanent after she graduates. Again, internships are low cost, low risk ventures for most companies. They are justified as a source of future employees and community goodwill. Most CEO's love aggressive young people and will respond graciously to cold calls from college students who are eager to learn and gain experience.

Negotiating Terms

While it is very important to pick the right internships, the terms of your employment are virtually irrelevant. You will find that some internships pay and some don't. If you need to make money, your choices will be more limited. Be aware that payment (or non-payment) is probably non-negotiable. Unlike the real job you'll be chasing after graduation, the terms will be "take it or leave it." On the other hand, the days of the week and hours you work are generally flexible. Having a great company listed on your résumé (with one or two meaty accomplishments) is very important, but it is doubtful that anyone will ever ask you how many hours a week you worked.

Establish Yourself Immediately

Keep in mind that your supervisor may have only hired you to win a few executive brownie points. If this is the case, you may not be given anything meaningful to do and thus fail to generate a future job opportunity or résumé grist. The best way to smoke this out and force your new boss to take you seriously is to complete everything they assign as fast as possible. Not only will they take notice, but they will also quickly realize that they can't invent enough busy work to keep you quiet for the next few months; they will have to actually let you help them do their job. It's important for you to strike quickly; ideally your first day on the job. The more time that expires before you're taken seriously, the greater the odds are that you'll be ignored.

Beef Up Your Meager Résumé

What's on your résumé; a job as camp counselor, or perhaps a stint flipping burgers? Perhaps a critical section where you reveal what sports you excelled in during high school? If you're like most young people, there's probably nothing on your résumé yet that will help you win your first real job, or even get you an interview. Your internship portfolio is the only chance you have to create accomplishments for your post-graduate résumé. To do this, you'll need project-type assignments, ideally with tangible results or at least an impressive report or presentation. If you work four to five internships during college and create two to three projects that you can list on your résumé and talk about in an interview, you'll have little difficulty landing your first real job.

Get A Letter

When the final weeks of your internship come around, the team will probably take you to lunch and maybe even give a little gift; after all, everyone loves kids. That's all wonderful, but you need to focus the last week of your internship on building references for your future. Don't be afraid to humbly ask co-workers and supervisors if you can use them for a reference—they're expecting it. Once they say yes, make sure you get private contact information (home and cell phone numbers, private email address, etc.) and ask them for a letter of reference. Offer to draft the letter, welcome their edits, and then get them to sign it. Nothing says "I'm a future winner" to a potential employer like a handful of articulate letters of reference. This also eliminates the risk that you lose track of your references in years to come, or worse, they forget who you are.

Ask About The Future

The final step is to ask your supervisor if they'd be willing to discuss a full time job after graduation. They may be a little uneasy about this and qualify their answer with something like, "assuming we have an opening and assuming there's a good fit," but that's okay. Anyone who tells you they can offer you a job a year or two from now is probably delusional. The important thing is to open the dialog and make a strong enough impression that they'll remember you favorably if and when you call after graduation.

Internships are easy to secure and painless to complete. The only big mistake you can make is to fail to go after them. Complete several before the spring of your senior year and you won't have to grovel to land your first real job.

Profile Hayley St. Philip

Conquering the Afterlife (of college that is)

Hayley St. Philip considers herself fortunate. She has wonderful parents, a great family and friends, and most of all, she succeeds at almost everything she attempts. After high school in the posh San Diego suburb of Del Mar, Hayley had the grades and the wherewithal to attend Pepperdine University in beautiful Malibu California. As a freshman she rushed for one of the most prestigious sororities in the country—Delta Gamma—and by her junior year she was elected president.

Hayley enjoyed working and always found great summer jobs. The summer before her senior year she worked for the ultimate fashion retailer—Nordstrom selling top clothing. But, to a certain extent, the grace with which Hayley navigated her young life may have hurt her. Since things always came relatively easy to Hayley, she was almost blindsided by one of life's biggest challenges—finding her first real job.

Hayley aspired to a career in sales and marketing, like her dad, but never thought seriously about where she'd work after graduation. It was the fall of her senior year and she had never had an internship. She knew there were a myriad of different vocations within the field of marketing, but she had no idea which one was for her. She was also clueless about where she'd work. Her dad had worked in pharmaceuticals, but she didn't think she wanted to do that. She didn't really want to move back to San Diego, but LA was a big scary place. Time was running out and the "afterlife" was closing in fast.

In December before her last semester of college, she got an email from a professor about internship opportunities at Fox Broadcasting Company, "Work on the next American Idol, 24, Family Guy, etc..." It immediately caught Hayley's attention. The whole idea of working in the entertainment field had never occurred to Hayley, but she is a long time fan of American Idol and thought it might be an interesting experience. The thought of working with the next Carrie Underwood or Jack Bauer in person sent tingles up her spine.

Hayley applied, got an interview and landed the internship in the Publicity Department at FOX Broadcast. Within her first week at FOX she was intrigued by the people, the environment and became passionate about working there fulltime. She immediately started "auditioning" to everyone she met. After graduation, she decided to continue her internship to help work the Idol finale, but to also show her dedication and interest in the company. She continued to win over everyone she met. After the finale, the Senior Vice President of the department asked Hayley to fill in as a temp for a week while her assistant was going to be away. Hayley knew this was an important time to distinguish herself as a potential employee versus just an intern. Timing was on her side because at the end of that month, a job as a Photo Publicity Assistant opened up. Hayley was asked to interview and she landed her first job out of college. She quickly said goodbye to summer as she formerly knew it and headed off to work in June. She continued to prove herself in the department and in September that same executive who she temped for back in May asked her to be her new coordinator in publicity. Hayley seized the phenomenal opportunity and was thankful for the promotion as she knew this would open her up to more in the future. In

November of 2007 she was asked to take over the FOX intern program. She immediately expanded the program beyond Los Angeles and is currently managing 6 top interns from across the country.

Although Hayley St. Philip entered the world of internships a little late, she has clearly made up for lost time. I met with her one sunny Sunday January morning in the desert of Southern California and she told me some of the most important lessons she has learned about having a successful internship.

Interns *Are* the New Hire Talent Pool
"When it came to finding our first job after college, we were really living in a dream world. We all figured good grades, a diploma from a great school, and a long list of impressive extracurricular activities would guarantee multiple job offers after graduation, man were we wrong. Once I got to FOX I learned that the intern program was their primary vehicle for finding new employees. They very seldom hired someone out of college who had not interned with them first.

The Internship Is the Interview
"A lot of kids think that an internship is just a way to dress up their résumé. They imagine that the simple fact that they worked during school at a real company will impress a potential employer. While it's true that people seldom complain if a non-paying intern doesn't do much, that doesn't mean you should just sleepwalk through your internship. Even if you're interning for a company that you're unlikely to work for after college, make sure you put on your best performance. And if you have even the slightest inkling that it's a place you'd like to go to after graduation, show them how good you are every minute you're there. Yes, there will be a formal interview before you get a bonafide job offer, but unless you sell them from day one, you'll never even get a chance. First impressions are the most lasting."

Hayley's Internship Etiquette 101

"Converting an internship into a full time job is not that difficult. Here are some quick ways to make sure people take notice and remember you later:

- Walk up to everyone, introduce yourself and shake their hand.

- Show curiosity, ask them about themselves, their job, and how they got where they are.

- Be ridiculously willing to do the most menial job.

- Never forget that you're on the bottom of the totem pole; it's a privilege to be an intern."

Be Supersensitive About Office Politics

"It sneaks up on you so fast. One minute you're just sitting around with a bunch of coworkers making small talk and suddenly someone starts to gossip about a person who's not there or even their boss. The next thing you know everyone's chipping in their own story. It's so easy to jump in and slam your boss, but you never know who you can trust. How would you feel if your boss heard your comment from someone else? My rule is never say something about anybody that you wouldn't say to their face."

This is Life's First Big Reality Check

"I was very lucky. I got my first internship and "converted" it to my dream job. A lot of kids aren't so lucky. I've been with FOX for over a year and I know people who graduated with me and still haven't found a job. This is your first brush with reality. We have pretty much lived in a cocoon up until now. We may not have been accepted by every college we applied to, but we were accepted somewhere. Your first job is way more difficult. You can apply to as many companies as you want, but if you're not someone they need, you'll never get an offer."

Don't Fear the Afterlife

"I can honestly say that I never met anyone in college who was afraid that they wouldn't get a job after graduation. Everyone's biggest fear is that they'll end up with a job they don't love. I have news for everyone, you may not end up with a job at all and your odds of getting a job you love right after you graduate are very slim. Your fear is legitimate, it's just misplaced. Conquer all fear before you get to the real world. Do yourself a big favor and start interning as soon as possible. Get four or five internships under your belt before your last semester. You'll not only find out first hand whether or not you like that kind of work, you'll get a big head start on landing your dream job before you graduate."

STRATEGY TWO

Select An Employer That Suits Your Nature

You may or may not have begun your first real job, but you've probably committed to a career direction. This doesn't mean that you can't modify your trajectory, but if you've got a degree in accounting, it may be tough to become an aerospace engineer without starting all over again. Still, there are a wide variety of employment options open to a degreed accountant. You can try and find a job close to home with a small firm, go to work for a major auditing company and see the world, start your own practice, or just hop on a plane to Maui; "because they must need accountants over there." At this point in your career, the decision you make about where to work is as important as any you'll make in your life.

If your job has long hours, frequent travel, or a long commute, there isn't going to be much time left at the end of the day for your family or friends. On the other hand, your job may be strictly nine-to-five, but if it pays peanuts, it will be impossible to own a good home, live in a nice community, and send your children to a decent college. All employment opportunities are not equal and that's why the second strategy in *Career Secret Sauce* is Select an Employer that Suits Your Nature.

23

My Path Was Circuitous

When I gave up my dream of being an architect at 22 and went to work for Data Terminal Systems, I launched my career on a materials management trajectory. I was 26 when I concluded that marketing, not manufacturing, was the field for me. Fortunately, I was working for a fast-growing, medium-sized company. I was able to transition into a supervisory job in sales administration and shift directions toward marketing. By age 34, I had a family and worked for Prime, a billion-dollar multinational corporation. This enabled me to move my young family to Europe to start up a new business under the security of a large company. I was 37 when I realized that the economy and climate in Massachusetts was not for me. After about 6 months I figured out a way to get Computervision (a Prime Company) to offer me a transfer to Silicon Valley in California. At 40, it hit me that big company politics were detrimental to my health. I quit Computervision and went to work in a smaller firm that was contemplating a public offering. I was 48 when I realized that being a CEO might not be fraught with the overwhelming burden of responsibility I had always feared, so I accepted the position with XPORTA, a struggling global trade services company in Santa Clara. And I was 52 when I left the software business and moved to the desert to become an author.

I easily could have done what most people do and spent my entire career in the same company (or industry, job, and community) that I began my career in. On the other hand, whenever my career seemed to stagnate, I chose to shake things up and change my field, relocate, or both. It's possible that I could have made better choices earlier in life and gotten to the place I'm now at much sooner, but I believe my courage to take risks is the reason I have enjoyed a successful career. Human inertia is a powerful force in life; most people never even consider changing employers, careers, or geographies until they're forced to do so. My family and I have enjoyed the good fortune of experiencing a variety of cultures, climates, and people, while still having time for living. We've made friends in many places and enjoyed stronger financial security than most of my associates who chose to stay in one place. I also believe that the breadth of experience I developed by moving around has made me a more qualified employee and ultimately enhanced my job security.

My brother-in-law Rudy worked for several years in material management before he decided, at age 28, to become a firefighter and then buy a chimney sweep business. He has never regretted that decision. Once I moved to California, I was amazed at the number of people I met who were born in the East or Midwest and moved West early in their career. Every one of them freely admitted that moving to California was one of the best career decisions they had ever made. While I love California, I suspect there are people out there who have moved to other regions and feel the same way. Most of this book is about things you can do within your current job to enhance your career success; including relocation. If your job is not working for you, radically changing employers or moving to the place you've always dreamt of is a great way to positively transform your life.

Where Are The Best Jobs In Your Industry Located?

The answer to this question is so obvious I can't believe that it took me over a decade to figure it out. In 1986, I thought that I had established a career in sales and marketing. Prime was struggling at the time, so I updated my résumé and started sniffing around for a better job. After a number of interviews that seemed to go well but yielded no offers, I realized what was happening. By working for Data Terminal Systems and then Prime Computer, I had inadvertently backed into an industry pigeonhole. I was not just a sales and marketing guy; I was a computer industry sales and marketing guy. I say inadvertent because I never consciously decided to become a computer marketing professional or even a high-tech worker—it just happened. When I went to work in 1976, the only new job openings in Massachusetts were with high-tech companies. After six years at Data Terminal

25

Systems and five years at Prime, I had become a de facto computer guy.

Once I figured this out, I knew why I was having a tough time finding a new job in Massachusetts. The computer industry in Massachusetts was floundering. The job openings I was applying for were either in high-tech areas other than computers or not high-tech at all. Armed with this realization, I ended up staying with Prime, but transferred into a sales job in the Computervision Division, which I later parlayed into a transfer to Silicon Valley, the high-tech capital of the universe. Once I moved to Silicon Valley, I never had a serious problem finding a job again.

If you begin your career where you grew up, you too may inadvertently pigeonhole yourself into the local industry and completely eliminate other career options. You can't have a career in marketing unless you live somewhere that has a company headquarters nearby that is big enough to have a marketing department. If marketing is your game, there better be more than one large company, or you will have to relocate later to get ahead. There are very large companies like Caterpillar or SAS Institute that are located in remote semi-rural areas, but they are rare. These companies do provide a broad range of job opportunities, but they also have a captive labor market. That's how they keep wages low.

While this seems quite intuitive, the fact is that this topic is tough to research in any depth or detail beyond the obvious anecdotal examples: investment in New York, automotive in Detroit, insurance in Hartford, and computers San Jose. An excellent source for researching this topic is the State Occupational Projections web site (www.projectionscentral.com/projhome.asp). It is a specialized search database based on the Bureau of Labor Statistics (BLS) from the U.S. Department of Labor and state projections developed from the labor market information sections of each State Employment Security Agency. Since it's based on BLS data, it has hundreds of job categories. Some are very general while others are quite specific. It enables a quick answer to questions like the following:

Question: What is the fastest growing white-collar job over the next 10 years by state and where is it located?

Answer: Network systems and data communications analysts in Idaho.

Question: What are the top 5 states for network systems and data communications analysts jobs in 2012?

Answer: New York, Texas, California, Pennsylvania, and Ohio.

Question: What's the job market in Arizona look like for Accountants and Auditors over the next ten years?

Answer: By 2012, there will be 24,100 accountant and auditor jobs in Arizona, up 25 percent from 19,270 in 2002.

You can combine the results of this web site with salary.com to also research what companies are paying in potential new locations.

Your Ideal Natural Habitat

If you're just getting started in your career, now is the best time to consider moving away or settling in near school or where you grew up. Once your career starts to take off, your options will be more limited. Right now you don't have a lot of furniture and you're accustomed to living in austere quarters like a dormitory. You're already separating from your friends at college and if you head back to your hometown, most of your high school friends have probably moved away. With any luck, your career may only give you binary options for job relocation later in life, but now you have the luxury of considering every possible option.

The thought of packing up and moving away may be too frightening to consider, but don't block it out. Invest some private time in researching potential venues and contemplate the possibility of relocating. There is a plethora of information sources and web sites to learn more about other parts of the country. I would recommend that you start at Money Magazine's Best Places to Live section and undertake some high level research (http://money.cnn.com/magazines/moneymag/bplive/2007/index.html—replace 2007 with the most recent calendar year). They spend a lot of time and money keeping it current and it has a great search engine for prioritizing what matters most to you. Once you have a short list of potential locales, cross-reference it with the Projection Central and salary.com to find the sweet spot between geography and opportunity for your chosen profession.

Finally, if you've already started your career and it's not going the way you planned, crank up these tools and see if there's a better place for you to work. In 2003, my PR agent, Monica Proctor, had an excellent career running her own agency out of Boulder, Colorado. Her hobby was jazz singing and there wasn't a whole lot of it happening there. She did some research and discovered that Austin, Texas had a great local music scene and a larger market for her services in PR. She rented her place in Boulder, packed up, drove to Austin, and started doing PR work there. As it turned out, she met the love of her life, got married, had a child and the last time I heard, is now living happily ever after.

Profile Ed Muzik
Finding His Ideal Environment

> Growing up in Chicago, Ed Muzik never thought much about weather as a kid. Weather was fairly overlooked and he got used to the idea that it would be lousy half the time. His passion for people fed into his desire to become a doctor to help others in need; however, life never goes quite as planned, and he ended up studying to become an electrical engineer. Like most college kids, Ed switched majors

midway through college and ultimately graduated with a degree in Finance and Accounting, enabling him to use his mathematical skills and still spend time with people.

One morning Ed's (first) wife suggested that they leave Chicago and head for a warmer climate. He shrugged off the idea at first, but as he trudged through the slush to get on a train to work he concluded, "Maybe we should look at moving somewhere sunny."

The Muziks quickly looked over various relocation options and narrowed the search down to San Diego or San Jose, both warm spots in California. Although San Diego had the initial edge, they ultimately selected San Jose due to the strong economy and the fact that Ed had family there.

The nice thing about a finance career is that it enables you to change industries much easier than in other vocations; Ed is living proof. He started in retail with Marshall Fields and moved to electronics in Chicago. He later arrived in San Jose unemployed, and ended up working in hi-tech and construction.

I met Ed in 2005 after he had remarried and moved to the desert of Southern California to work as CFO for the Hi-Desert Water District. Now Ed plays golf on weekends, gets every other Friday off, and will soon qualify for a government pension. He even made a recent run in local politics to become a member of the Water District Board of Directors. Although he did not win, perhaps he'll try again next time.

Ed is an excellent example of a person who made strategic career moves about where to work and who to work for, and ultimately found his dream job environment.

Recently Ed and I had lunch together and he shared the most significant epiphanies in his well-lived career:

If You Love Your Environment, Your Career Will Be Successful

"I never thought that there was anything wrong with Chicago, but once we figured out that we could live and work in a warm climate, we just had to get out of town. Obviously some people love Chicago and it works well for them. Others love the sun, hate the cold, and never do anything about it. My biggest piece of advice is to consider whether your current environment is adding to your career happiness or a nagging annoyance. Do you race to a different climate for vacations? When you return home do you dread going back to your job, or is it just something about where you work and live? Your problem could be simply your commute, or maybe you need to change your entire geographic region. Once we moved to San Jose, everything about my life changed. I loved the atmosphere of the Bay Area and that made me more productive at work. It was as if the sun and warmth was my reward for going to work."

For Quality of Life, Think Government

"If you want to catch every little league game, not worry about your retirement income, and have plenty of vacation time, you really ought to consider a public sector career. When I got to the Water District I was struck by the contrast between an entrepreneurial work environment and that of a public utility. It was like night and day. You'll never get rich working for the government, but you'll sure avoid a lot of life's work related anxieties. Of course, in a lot of places in this country, you can't afford to live on a public sector income. If this is the career environment you're looking for, the trick is to find a job in a place with a low cost of living."

For Money and Action, Follow a Local Entrepreneur

"In San Jose, I went to work for a small company involved in selling capital equipment for tax shelters. The fellow who started the company was a natural born entrepreneur with a knack for finding creative new ways to make money. The work was fun and we all made good money. If the business got in trouble, he just took off for Hawaii to clear his head. In two weeks, he'd be back with a bunch of fresh ideas and the next thing I knew we were making piles of money doing something completely different. Most cities have hidden pockets of opportunity that you don't learn about in college. In San Jose, it was real estate and cars. A good entrepreneur in either of these businesses could help you tap into an endless stream of wealth opportunities. If money is your thing and you don't know how you're going to pull it off, look around for an entrepreneur with a good handle on how to make money in your city and he or she will show you where to find the money."

Of course, your career change doesn't have to be as dramatic as Ed Muzik's. If the organization you work for is big enough, you can often transition to a new vocation through two or three lateral job transfers. I went from production control to sales administration to marketing within the same company over the course of two years. The important thing is being aware that every career has different work and lifestyle characteristics associated with it and if you're less than thrilled with your current job, you may have simply ended up working at the wrong place. If you think that's a big part of your career problem, you can start taking steps to fix it right away.

The first step toward improving your situation is to understand the options for where you might work and consider the lifestyle characteristics associated with each option before making your decision. Career Secret Sauce is about what you can do on your current job to enhance your satisfaction, compensation, freedom, and job security. These techniques will help you regardless of where you work, but if you're working in the wrong place it may overpower all of the other job satisfaction factors.

Does The Nature Of The Employer Suit Your Nature?

Once you've gotten in sync with the regional and industry factors for your chosen career, you can look at your employer's organization and see if it offers a work environment you can thrive in. Some organizations offer virtual lifetime job security; others pay better or have more opportunities for advancement or career change.

31

There are also companies that are just more fun to work at. Your individual strengths may be more valuable in one organization than another. Big organizations need sophisticated administrative skills like accounting, personnel, legal, or facilities management. You won't find many jobs calling for these skills in small companies. As a rule, small companies prefer people with broad skills who don't get upset with constantly changing priorities. Government organizations and big companies tend to want people who follow procedures and don't make waves. Consider how important these factors are to you and figure out if your current or prospective employer appreciates your style or finds it annoying. You may discover that simply working for an organization that complements your personal work philosophy could be your Career Secret Sauce.

The Sparkle Of A Big Company Can Be Deceiving

The quest for job security can cloud our thinking when it comes to career decisions. This is particularly true when it comes to company size. We are taught early that big companies are safer places to work. They have more money, more facilities, more customers, and, most of all, they've been around a lot longer than smaller companies. If you think that you might want to work in a big company, make it your first job out of college. Most of them like to hire young new employees before they get "contaminated" by working elsewhere. Big companies play the numbers game, so they usually want the top students from the best schools. If you're a college senior, it can be very flattering to be recruited by an IBM, Citibank, or Accenture.

In 1978 I was running Sales Administration at Data Terminal Systems and one of my subordinates hired a talented young woman who had just left a very large computer company. She had been with them for two years after being aggressively recruited during her senior year at an Ivy League college. She wanted to be in marketing, but this large prestigious firm told her, "everyone in marketing starts in sales." Accordingly, she entered their new hire sales program, which groomed salespeople by

32

teaching them how to sell small ticket items to companies with few employees (like typewriters to insurance agents). After two years, she was less than spectacular at selling and her future in marketing was beginning to tarnish. Then the big computer company had a minor sales miss for the quarter, and lay-offs followed. She was cut.

Of course, she never actually met anyone at that big company who could have hired her in marketing, and therefore, no one had ever been able to evaluate her marketing talent. She wasn't fired because of her lack of marketing skill; she lost her job simply because the new hire program had to reduce its headcount. They got rid of the least promising salespeople (i.e. those who sold the fewest typewriters in their first two years), and she was one of them. As a marketing professional, I know that this is probably the toughest field to enter straight out of college, but getting there through a big company's new hire sales program is very risky.

Suppose she had been great at selling typewriters? She might have won some awards, landed bonuses, been given bigger accounts, and maybe have even been placed in a sales manager trainee program. It is unlikely that would have helped her with her marketing career. Her boss, likely a career sales professional, would have wanted her to stay in sales. Sales managers never want to lose good salespeople and her dreams of being a marketeer may have evaporated.

The same is true for other vocations in big companies. Accounting departments hire young CPAs (Certified Public Accountants) and if they turn out to be good, they don't want to share them with the treasury department. After 18 months in Production Control at DTS, I applied for a job in Sales Administration doing order scheduling. My former boss invited me over to his house for dinner to talk me out of it. Then, his boss laid out a two-year plan for me that would have doubled my salary if I only stayed in Production Control. Fortunately, I was working for a small company and the people in sales who were recruiting me had the political strength to pressure my old department to let me go. Bigger companies have politics too, but it's tougher to figure out who has the political power, particularly early in your career.

Of course, big companies do have a lot more career opportunities and once you've established a strong track record, figured out the political landscape, and made the right political connections, they're good places to move around in. But this movement will take decades and the longer you stay at a big company the harder it is to leave. Other big companies don't want you because you didn't come through their system and you don't know their procedures and policies. Smaller companies don't want you because they're afraid that you won't be able to get things done without the support system that a big company provides.

By now you may have figured out that your chances of joining a big company will be very limited later in your career so you do have to make this choice early. If you have been working for a few years and can't seem to get an interview at a big company, don't beat yourself up. It's not you, it's them. Big companies don't hire many people who have been trained elsewhere.

None of this is meant to say that big companies are bad; they simply have their own unique way of developing employee talent. If you're looking for a regimented career with established career paths, long term job security, great health plans, and retirement benefits—and you don't want to change employers for the rest of your career—a big company may be the right place for you to go. Of course, if you want to work fewer hours and you can get by on less money, perhaps you should be thinking about a public sector career instead.

The Sanctuary Of The Public Sector

It is true that a career in the public sector is very secure. It's virtually impossible to get fired for anything short of criminal behavior. A union negotiates your annual salary increase, and despite recent grumblings, your retirement income and benefits are the best you can get. This may sound great, but there are pros and cons worth considering when it comes to a public sector career. Moreover, not all public sector careers are the same.

Over the years, the security blanket provided by public sector employment has migrated from supplying job, pay, and retirement security to providing a complete career cocoon. It may be nice not having to grovel for your next raise, but it is also a little depressing to know that no matter how hard you work, your salary or chances for potential promotion will be identical to the sluggish clock-puncher down the hall. If you're a teacher and you want more money, get a masters or PhD. Learning a second language may get you a bump in pay, but if the only thing you do well is turn out smarter kids, your pay will remain the same. If you're a policeman or a firefighter, take a test. The person with the highest score gets his name on the top of the list for the next promotion. You may earn additional points for being a veteran or putting in years on the job, but your performance at work will have virtually nothing to do with getting a promotion or a raise.

This blindness in hiring and promotions can be a great benefit, if you're a minority and find it tough to crack the private sector. My father-in-law, Herbey Vaillancourt, was a French Canadian growing up in Fitchburg, Massachusetts, when the Irish ruled the roost. After fighting in the Philippines and earning two Purple Hearts and a Bronze Star during World War II, he returned to town as a war hero. Unfortunately, the Irish didn't care much for the French Canadians, and, despite his war record, Herbey had a hard time finding work. He took a civil service test and did rather well, earning extra points with his outstanding military record. He landed a job with the US Post Office, where he worked his entire life; he went on to become a City Councilor in Fitchburg and to own and operate a couple of small businesses in town.

Affirmative Action cuts both ways. My firefighter friends tell me that it has become extremely difficult to get into the department if you're a Caucasian male. Hiring and promotions are based on a point system, and minorities are awarded extra points to help them win jobs. Candidates without these extra points have to score at the very top of their class to get a starting job. You may or may not think this is fair, but it is a fact of modern life and something to consider. If you're not a member of a minority group, affirmative action programs may make it tough to find employment in the public sector. On the other hand, if you do qualify, this may be a great place for you to work. Objective testing and union negotiated benefits will enable you to avoid potential racial prejudice that could limit your career down the road. The same dynamic is beginning to emerge in very big companies, but to a lesser degree.

There is another angle to consider when evaluating a career in the public sector: the job choices themselves are different. Obviously, police or firefighting jobs are virtually exclusive to the public sector. Teaching positions are available in both private and public sector organizations, as are accounting and other administrative jobs. There are also plenty of science and engineering opportunities working for the government. Depending on what you enjoy, you may or may not find a public service career option.

Of course, not all public sector careers are the same. If you think corporate promotions and raises are all about politics and prefer an objective system for advancement, the public sector might be ideal for you. On the other hand, if you crave feedback and welcome competition in your life and career, you may find it quite frustrating. There are jobs in the public sector that do have feedback and competition, but it's not always tied to compensation. Elected officials, soldiers, prosecutors, and police detectives certainly have positions that involve winning, losing, and frequently competing. In addition, they offer the ability to crisscross back and forth between the public and private sectors.

Another option is to do what my firefighter friends do and consider creating a hybrid career that is half public service and half private sector entrepreneur. Police officers, firefighters, and schoolteachers, among others, often take this track. Perhaps you want to take off three days a week, or even the whole summer, and you don't need much money to live on. A public service job might be your ticket to the life you want. The point is there are numerous options in the public sector that go beyond simply punching a clock with bulletproof job security and lifetime benefits. While policemen and firefighters risk their lives at work, the career most risk-seekers frequently choose is within the small entrepreneurial company.

Small Companies Are Just Plain Fun

If big companies and government work makes you feel like a number, the other end of the career spectrum may be your best bet. Small companies invented casual Fridays and "bring your pet to work" days. Everyone knows everybody and it often feels like one big family.

While small businesses offer virtually none of the job security benefits of the large organizations previously discussed, they do offer a different kind of personal security that comes from being known as a person, not just a badge number. When I took over XPORTA, it was a small company with very little cash in the bank. Yet, I was able to recruit former associates to join us with a simple promise: "As long as I have a job here, you'll have a job here." Small companies are a particularly great place for an experienced worker who is tired of being lost in a big company and is seeking a non-political environment that respects him for what he can do.

One of the best things about working for a small business is the mobility you have to try different work roles. For example, you may be the bookkeeper, but the boss needs someone to run an ad in the local paper and voila, you're a marketeer. If you're not sure what you really want to do, or simply want a lot of variety in your job, a small business might be a fun place to work.

When you work for a small business, your rewards are often more closely tied to the success of the company. Shortly after I joined Data Terminal Systems in 1976, the CEO, Bob Collings, announced that every time we doubled our profits all employees and their spouses would go on a one-week, all expenses paid vacation to some exotic destination. The program was so unique that it landed us a center spread in Fortune magazine. We went on to double profits three or four times and each time we did everyone went on vacation together. We also had a quarterly bonus program and a stock option plan for everyone in the company. As a young executive in my first job, this was great. I felt like I was part of a team and I was highly motivated to help the company win, as were most employees—even the janitors. Unfortunately, all good things do end.

In 1980, the big companies we had been winning market share from woke up and started to compete with us in earnest. We missed a quarter, lost a ton of money, and suddenly there were no company paid vacations, no bonuses, and too many layoffs to keep track of (including me). When you work for a small business, you are a lot closer to the action, which is beneficial when things are going well and risky when they aren't. The trick is to join a small company just before they start to expand and then head for greener pastures at the first sign of trouble. Small businesses have very little staying power. When things start to go bad, they seldom ever get better.

It's okay to have a personal life in a small business, but it is often intertwined with your work life. Collings knew that DTS employees would have to sacrifice personal time in order for the company to succeed and created a very family friendly incentive plan to help "soften the blow" at home. That's why he invited spouses on the company vacation trips.

If you or your spouse gets sick while working for a small business, the odds that the company will help you out, or at least cut you some slack, are much higher than in larger organizations. You also need to have a spouse and family who enjoy company events. Small businesses have frequent social events and spouses are expected to show up at every one of them; family support is important with small business careers.

In the last few decades, big companies and government organizations have started to bend over backwards to be fair to their employees. Diversity training, sexual harassment policies, etc., have become the law of the land. Small businesses, however, haven't quite caught up. Most often, small businesses are started by a group of like-minded individuals who leave a larger company out of frustration to want to try business on their own. The problem with like-minded groups is that they're often alike in more ways than one: all white men, all women, or all members of a certain race or ethnic group. It's probably not intentional; it's just the way it happened. Starting a new business is fraught with risk. People naively assume that they can reduce risk by sticking with people they know, and invariably, that creates an environment light in diversity. I believe most people are naturally open-minded, however, and eventually they realize that their exclusionary employment practices are wrong and actually limiting the talent pool they can draw from to build their business. If you're not from their group, but hit them at the moment they decide it's time to become more inclusive, you may discover a great opportunity and a unique life experience.

While intra-company romance is generally frowned upon in large companies and government offices, this is seldom the case in small companies. The long hours, younger workforce, and family atmosphere of small businesses tend to nurture these amorous relationships and make it impossible to keep them a secret. The line between sexual harassment and flirtation are a lot grayer and the odds of being asked out on a date by your boss are greater. These instances are not guaranteed to happen; they're just more likely to within a smaller company. Of course, if you're looking for love and plan to work long hours, that small company environment may enable you to kill two birds with one stone!

The best thing about working for a small business is the opportunity it provides to "hitch your wagon to a star". Without all of the politics and bureaucracy of a large company, it is much easier to spot the company all-stars who are destined to have great careers. This environment enables you to get to know these future leaders, work for and with them, and even join them when they move on to something better down the road.

Working for a small company is exciting, but it also makes it difficult to have a private life outside of work. It may end up that work is so much fun that you don't care, but be cautious if you have a spouse and children who want to do things differently. Working for small business is seldom a casual employment.

The Path To Rapid Advancement—Midsize Growth Companies

Somewhere in between the very large, stable, multinational companies and the small struggling businesses lie a number of companies that represent what I consider the best of both worlds. These companies are big enough to survive a weak economic cycle, yet small enough to enable you to enjoy career mobility. The actual size of a midsize company will vary by industry, but generally they're big enough to be known in their marketplace, but young enough to adapt to new trends. Generally, these companies have hundreds, not tens of thousands, of employees.

If you're just starting your career, a midsize company will provide you with the opportunity to demonstrate your abilities and reward your performance with rapid promotions and raises. Since they are growing, they will

40

get bigger as your career blossoms and thus create more room for you near the top. Experienced workers will also benefit from these companies. They generally don't care where you worked in the past; as long as you have a skill they need they'll give you a chance to prove yourself.

Companies this size have the critical mass necessary to operate without the Herculean might and weekend contributions that small companies often demand from their employees. Odds of having a successful career and working less than 50 hours a week are much better here than in a small business. While these companies have a few social events a year, it is less noticeable if you don't show up or you come without your family. These companies are serious businesses, not alternative family units.

Unlike small businesses, midsize companies have jobs that will translate well on your résumé when the day comes to move on. Many of these companies have publicly traded stock, which means that they have to be run by standard practices and procedures. They are also likely to have employee stock ownership and stock option programs available for building long term wealth. In small businesses, the owner and/or their family own everything. Big businesses often have stock purchase plans, but because of their size, the stock price appreciates very slowly. Two of the three midsize growth companies I worked for had spectacular stock appreciation over a four year period. The key is knowing when to sell.

Companies this size are often big enough to have department hierarchies. At Data Terminal Systems in 1978, I was promoted to Manager of Sales Administration. I reported to the Director of Marketing Administration and I had three supervisors who reported to me. Each of them could see at least two career moves ahead of them and I could see at least one. Changing companies is never fun, so having room for promotion in your current job is a definite plus.

You can also traverse departments more easily, as I did when I moved from manufacturing into sales and marketing. Manufacturing was the only job I could get right out of college; Marketing was never a consideration. Once I got into the company and I saw how it operated, I realized that marketing was where I wanted to be. Because of the company's size, the managers in marketing knew who I was and gave me a chance.

This is another beautiful thing about midsize companies: you can actually get to know the top managers of the firm, despite your lesser position in the hierarchy. Once they know you, you can earn a reputation that leads to promotions both within and across departments. This visibility provides a certain job security that comes from being a known player. It's very difficult to achieve this in a large organization.

Finally, companies this size are often ideal takeover candidates for bigger companies. On the surface, a takeover sounds grim. It can be if you're near the top of the organization, but if you're in the middle, it can be an opportunity. The acquiring company is almost always desperate to make the acquisition succeed. They hope that the senior executives will stick around and make it work, but most of the top brass move on as fast as they can. Middle managers who commit to the new parent company become the new key employees for making the merger succeed. If you can get yourself into a situation like this, you can fast forward your career several years by helping the acquiring company integrate your old company. Most middle managers who do this are rewarded with rapid promotions in the larger parent company.

Where you chose to work can be the most powerful influence on your career satisfaction. Consider all factors before you jump into your first job. If you're already working, take the time to examine your current employer and how well your job situation meets your lifestyle objectives. If it doesn't match up well, change where you work and find a place that complements your values and career goals.

PHASE TWO

Create a Reputation as a Future Winner

STRATEGY THREE

Thrive On Your New Job

There is a very special feeling that comes with walking through the front door to your first real job. It's a blend of anxiety and excitement about "what's to come" combined with the realization that you may be doing it over and over again for years to come. New jobs are daunting, whether you're fresh out of school or an experienced manager coming in to take over a troubled department. How you handle the first few weeks in your new position will often determine your success or failure. Do it right, and you'll set yourself up for both promotions and future job opportunities. Fumble around, send the wrong signals, make enough rookie mistakes, and you'll most likely crash and burn within the first two years.

The first months on a new job are like none other in your career. The nature of work will likely be strange, as you'll start off doing nothing productive and having to learn everything all at once. You will be secretly studied by your boss, coworkers, and, if you have any, your subordinates. You will be initially forgiven for your ignorance, burdened with the obligation to respect all sorts of rituals and things you don't yet understand, and constantly measured on how fast you're coming up to speed. In the vast majority of employment situations, your ability to succeed will be determined by how well you play the new guy game in those initial months. In order to win, you must quickly

understand the expectations of all of the major con-
stituents in the organization and then consistently surpass
them.

Your new job is also where you will start to build or extend
your personal career network. You will have the best
opportunity to make important new friends during this
time or accidentally alienate others. This is probably the
most important long-term component in your new
assignment.

Find Out Your Objectives *Before* You Accept

There are a number of do's and don'ts for the first few
months of your new job, but the biggest pitfall often
comes from failing to fully understand your initial
objectives. There are a variety of causes for this problem,
but regardless the source, you're the one who will suffer if
you let it happen to you. How do you end up with a job
without knowing your objectives? The person who hired
you may have neglected to tell you exactly what he
expected you to accomplish. Or he may have told you, but
you were so busy selling him that you didn't hear. Perhaps
he told you his objectives, but they weren't the same ones
shared by his boss or the rest of the company. Worst yet,
perhaps he has no objectives, he's just hiring you and
hoping you'll figure out what to do on your own! The point
is, this is the most critical information you will need to
know to get your new job off to a successful start, and you
must make sure you have it before the first day at work. In
fact, you should get it before you accept the position. The
best time to gather this information is at the end of the
interview cycle and before you confirm acceptance of your
job offer.

The Ultimate Value Of The Interview

A lot of people think that the only thing that matters in a
job interview is whether or not you get hired. While an
interview that doesn't result in an offer can't do much for
your career, the ultimate value of an interview is to figure
out if you can succeed at the job in question and how to
do so.

48

The interview process is a world unto itself. There are hundreds, if not thousands, of books dedicated to the topic of improving your chances of success in a job interview. It is a complicated subject and not one of my specialties. If you're looking for tactical interviewing skills, I recommend studying a couple of books devoted to this subject. One of my favorites is Paul Power's "Winning Job Interviews." It deals with the mental side of the process as well as providing very practical how-to's. Paul brings humor to a very dry and serious topic.

I am not a strong interviewee because after my first job, the rest of my career opportunities came through referrals from my personal network. We'll delve into referral interviews in Strategy Nine: In Search of Greener Pastures, but for now just keep in mind that a referral interview is one where an associate helps you get the interview and your foot is already halfway through the door before the questions and answers begin. Whether I was on a cold interview or a referral, I always did a fair amount of selling in the beginning of the interview. Once I felt they were interested, I would probe them about their objectives for the person they would ultimately be hiring.

Here are some of the questions I'd ask during the interview cycle and when I'd ask them (these questions apply to both the hiring manager and other people you might interview with along the way):

Early In The Interview Cycle

- Is this a new job, or would I be replacing someone?

- If this is new, why was this job created?

- If I'd be a replacement, what happened to the person who had the job last?

- How do you define success for the person you hire?

Later In The Cycle

- How much interaction do you like to have with people who report to you?

- Who do I interact with, who must I rely on to get my job done, and who must I provide service to?

- Do you prefer subordinates who ask permission before they take action, or those who take prompt action and seek "forgiveness" after the fact?

After The Offer, Before Acceptance

- How will you measure my performance?

- Will we have written objectives? If so, how often are they discussed and updated?

- What happens if we disagree on an objective or my performance?

- How do you provide positive feedback? How do you provide negative feedback?

- How long do you think I'll be in this job before I'm eligible for a promotion?

- Assuming I do well, what is the most likely career path in this job?

- What is the typical annual raise for a very successful employee in this position?

Finally, there are a number of questions which are almost never asked, but which can have a profound impact on your job satisfaction.

- Where will I be sitting? Do I have an office or a cubical?

- What are your typical office hours? Do we ever come in on weekends?

- What kind of computer or other equipment do you provide?

- Will I have administrative support?

- What are your travel policies?

That last one is a funny one. I once worked for a small company that had an informal policy to cheat airlines by double booking reservations. The trick was to buy a cheap paper ticket for a flight at least 30 days out from the day of travel and then make an identical last minute e-ticket reservation for the same flight for the trip you wanted to take (at full fare of course). When you showed up for the flight, you handed the desk attendant the paper ticket, they looked up your name, and hopefully they gave you a boarding pass using the lower priced paper ticket. The full fare e-ticket reservation simply deleted itself since you never showed up to claim it and your credit card was issued a refund.

This "travel policy" worked until the first employee got busted and lost his frequent flyer privileges. To be honest, the whole idea never sat well with me. It was unsettling to think of cheating the airline, the company that ultimately held my life in their hands for the duration of the flight.

The point is that if you're in a field with a lot of travel, you need to know how tight the new company's travel policy is before you take the job. Travel policies are usually etched in stone with few exceptions. On one hand, there are companies that expect employees to fly nights and weekends, take the cheapest flight available (regardless of the number of stopovers), and share rooms with coworkers in cheap motels. Other companies let employees pick their preferred airlines, schedule convenient flights, take non-stops wherever possible, and even permit business class for longer flights. Wouldn't you like to know which work environment you're going into before you accept the offer?

Along the same vein, one of the worst hires I ever made asked me a question after I had made him an offer and actually tipped me off to the fact that he would be a disaster. He asked me "Does this job have a lot of travel?" The job was in international industry marketing and as such, it was the most ridiculous question anyone could ask. I was so caught off guard that I said something like "the usual amount." I then cringed inside and quickly concluded that there was no practical way to rescind the job offer. Looking back, I should have immediately probed into the root of his question. It turned out that he was a Class A prima donna and needed weeks to prepare for any kind of a business trip. During the time preceding any business trip, he would continuously approach me with reasons why the trip was unnecessary. He only lasted about a year, but it was a painful 12 months.

Unfortunately, most people see the interview as a one-dimensional proposition. They either "win" the job, or they lose. You obviously want to get a solid offer on every opportunity that comes along, but if you neglect to ask these questions or carefully evaluate the answers, you'll never know if an opportunity is really good or bad for you until it's too late. Further, every answer you get provides you with a stepping-stone to success in your new job. If you understand what's expected of you, how you'll be measured, and the rewards of success before you start your new career venture, you'll be ready to make the most out of the ever-so-critical first 30 days.

The Ever So Critical First 30 Days

No reasonable person expects a newly hired professional to be a productive contributor on their first day on the new job. An engineer might get a project to work on within the first week, but his initial work is not likely to be used in a real product. A salesman or a service representative might go a month before he's even allowed to talk to a customer on his own. It's as if there is an invisible calendar counting down the days until you're no longer a new hire and while this varies by profession, I like to use 30 days as the benchmark.

During the first 30 days, there are virtually no stupid questions. You can ask about company history, people, products, customers, competitors and even folklore. Of course, the people who matter—your boss, coworkers, and subordinates—will be subconsciously monitoring your progress, so don't ask the same question more than two or three times. They will be impressed with the little things you pick up on day one, and concerned if you're still in the dark on anything important after the first month. They will pay more attention to the trend line than the questions themselves, so it's important to become a little more job savvy every day.

My Little Black Book

I start every new job with a blank spiral notebook. Inside the cover, I write down the objectives I learned during the interview cycle. On the pages inside, I record everything I learn while working the new assignment, no matter how trivial. I also write down questions I need answered as soon as they pop in my head. Once I learn the answer, I write it down and the name of the person who gave it to me. I don't wait until the first day on the job to start this process; as soon as I've accepted a new assignment, I begin feverishly mining information about the company. When I went to work at Aspect Development as the Vice President of Marketing, I asked a senior subordinate to send me a copy of everything they gave a new sales person when they started work. A few days later a package arrived at my house with thousands of pages of collateral. Not only did I have plenty to study before my first day, but I also realized that my top priority would be to simplify training for new salespeople! No one could possibly assimilate all of that material and confidently apply it to a sales situation. Today, most companies have internal web sites that are overloaded with training material. Ask to get access to it as soon as you accept the new job and make it a point to absorb as much as possible as fast as you can.

Every morning I'd open my notebook, review the objectives page and start writing down new questions and initial ideas for achieving and clarifying them. Or, I would simply break them down into bite-sized pieces that I could act on. It is amazing how ideas for improvement will jump out at you when you're new to a situation. For some reason, it's much harder to see new opportunities once you've been assimilated into an organization. During the first month, I'd arrange to sit down with my manager every few days and talk about what I'm learning. The notebook made it easy for me to tell him whom I'd met with, what they told me, and most importantly, I'd float new ideas about how to achieve the objectives he assigned. It also enabled me to show him that I was organized, self-motivated, and a structured thinker.

The end of the ever-so-critical first 30 days is also somewhat magical. It can happen subconsciously, like the first time you meet someone new on the job and you do not introduce yourself as a new employee. If you're in a customer facing position, it happens the first time you talk to a customer alone. It also ends the first time you go back to your boss with a real work plan, or an actual work product. From that point forward, forget about being forgiven for your ignorance—those days are over.

Profile Gary McGrath
Master of New Environments

Gary McGrath was fortunate to grow up in rural New Hampshire. His parents raised him with a rock solid value system and he was able to attend a great college, The University of New Hampshire, at in-state tuition rates. Gary is a classic Type A personality. He began his career in sales peddling ski equipment in Laconia, New Hampshire during high school. Recognizing that Lake Winnipesauke was a long way from the big city, he headed south after graduation and landed a job selling computer supplies in Cranston, Rhode Island. Although his technical skills were light, he made up for it with sheer tenacity, opening 256 new accounts during his first year. From there he went to work for NECCO, selling the first versions of personal computers to law firms.

Gary then parlayed this success into a job offer from Hewlett Packard. Although this meant changing companies for the third time in his young career, HP was considered a first class company and it opened up a breadth of future opportunities. Gary knew he would learn a lot at HP and it would add a great highlight to his résumé. Life was good there; he made more money, bought a lot of rapidly appreciating HP stock and, most importantly, met his wife, Amy, and got married.

One day he looked around and noticed that a hot little start-up company named Lotus had just gone public. He heard about salespeople making more money on stock options than commissions and concluded, "I've got to get me some of that."

At age 27, he had already built a network of headhunters and told them that he would "be willing to look outside HP for another Lotus." A year later he found what he'd was looking for and took a job with a hot young company called Banyan Systems. Gary was the third salesman the company hired and struck it rich in both commissions and stock incentives. His rapid career growth and personal success story earned him a feature profile in the Boston Globe Business Section.

Gary and I met a few years later. He was on his fifth or sixth job by then and he had focused exclusively on start-up companies with breakthrough technology. A pattern emerged: He loved the thrill of the hunt, learning new technology and markets, launching new products, meeting new people. He also had a habit of blowing away people by exceeding their initial expectations of his abilities. He spent his first year in a new job learning and making a name for himself. He'd sell like crazy in his second year, but often by the third year he'd either get bored or decide that the company wasn't going to make it. From there, he'd move on to the next new thing. Today Gary is on his tenth or eleventh company (who's counting?) and he has become an expert at being a new employee.

Recently we got together and he shared some of his secrets for success as the consummate new kid on the block:

Be a Savage Listener
"As soon as I think I may be interviewing for a job, I start interviewing them. I ask probing questions about the company and them as people. Right off the bat, they start thinking of me as a good listener."

Revisit The Interview
"In the weeks following my first day on the job, I make it a point to go back to everyone I interviewed with and review the things we talked about. I delve into the topics we discussed superficially in the initial interview and try to learn more about their thoughts and opinions. Here's the killer: I bring along a tape recorder and record the interview. People always remember the tape recorder and realize that I'm not a stereotypical salesman. I'm serious about my work. I'm a professional."

Be The Surprise Inside The Crackerjacks Box
"People say salesmen have 30 days to prove their worth. I don't think they have that long. I have always made a point of exceeding expectations and get out of the "new guy box" as soon as possible. People expect me to sell; that's what they hired me for. I try to go beyond selling and demonstrate additional value to the company. It could be in marketing or simply facilitating a new relationship that has nothing to do with selling. I do believe that salespeople have a "reputation equity bank" that they build up when times are good and draw down when they miss a sales goal. I start making deposits on day one."

Be A Human Being
"Almost everyone thinks salespeople are loud-mouthed, shallow mercenaries who only care about the size of their commission check. I make it my business to break that stereotype immediately. I keep

my mouth shut until I have something positive to contribute, I am genuinely interested in the people I work with, and I try to inject humor into life's little situations as often as I can."

Prepare For The Worse, Hope For The Best
"September 11 was even more devastating for salespeople than it was for everyone else. Suddenly, all budgets were frozen and none of my customers could conduct a rational discussion about ever buying anything again. I had a wife and four kids to feed; it was a scary time. I will never forget the feeling that I couldn't sell anything and it was beyond my control. Since then, I've worked every day like it's September 10, 2001 and I may not be able to sell a thing tomorrow."

Building Relationships—This is Your Personal Career Network

Another thing that occurs during your first 30 days is that you meet a lot of new people; in fact, just about everyone is new. The first time you meet someone is probably the only time you can politely tell them all about yourself without sounding conceited, so have a well-thought-out short biography queued up and ready on demand. It's also the only time you can ask a complete stranger to tell you their life story. This is the best way to build your own personally annotated organization chart. Ask people what they do; who they work for, how long they've been with the company, where they came from, or how to get things done around the office. Tell them the objectives you got from your boss and watch their reaction. Most of the time, their reaction will tell you something. They might say, "great, we need someone to do that," give you a sarcastic "good luck," or even just a snicker. If you get a lot of sarcastic good lucks or snickers, be on the alert; your boss may not have told you everything you need to know about your new job. Or, you may be simply bumping into your boss's political adversaries. Be friendly to all, but be cautious about making new friends just yet.

One of the recurring themes in *Career Secret Sauce* is the value of a close personal network. It is important to have coworkers who will watch your back, support your initiatives, bring you with them to new opportunities, and use their own network to help you if need a job. It may seem premature, but the first few months on your new job is the best time to size up people and subtly recruit them to become members of your personal network, as well as workplace friends. After six months, people will have formed opinions about you and it will be tougher to make a good first impression.

Befriend With Caution

I believe that our happiness in life depends on friendships and if we're spending 50+ hours a week on the job, it is essential to make friends at work. At the same time, our career success is greatly enhanced by carefully selecting the right friends. In many respects, friends at work are the same as friends anywhere. You want to build relationships with people you like and people who share your values and personal interests. I would never suggest you befriend someone at work who you would not have as a friend otherwise. At the same time, your on-the-job friends should also be contributing members of your personal career network, and never people who can jeopardize your reputation, so select with caution.

During the first few months on a job, it's difficult to figure out who your real friends will be. Your new boss may be quite friendly, but, in most cases he's just being temporarily social because he knows that you don't know anyone at the company. He may take you to lunch or even invite you out for a drink. This doesn't mean he wants to be your lifelong friend; he's just being a good people manager.

Peers are a little different. They may have political motives. They may seem to be reaching out because they want to be your new friend, but they're actually just pumping you for information. Watch out for questions with a hidden agenda. Often times peers will befriend you as a new hire just to figure out why you were really hired, if you're being paid more than they are, or if you might secretly be the next new boss.

Subordinates also realize that since you're new, you don't know anyone yet and they'll often reach out to become your new friend. Of course, they also know that it's just a matter of time before you become a real boss and they think you may go easier on them down the road if they butter you up now.

There are other candidates for friendship outside of your functional department. Most white-collar jobs involve serving one group and being served by others. If you're in marketing, you serve the sales department and are served, via new products, by the engineering department. If you're in manufacturing, you get orders from sales, materials from purchasing, and you are expected by everyone in the company to ship on time. You need to be careful about getting too friendly with people who serve you because it can make it tough to lean on them when you really need something. On the other hand, it's a very good idea to make friends with the people you serve. They can make life easy or difficult for you, and they are also your best source of references for a job well done.

Unfortunately, I have found no organizational template for building your personal network and deciding whom you want to make friends with. Rather than invent one, I recommend that you keep your eye out for people with certain winning traits and get to know them better. I've found that coworkers who possess these traits often make sincere friends and excellent members of your personal career network:

Well Connected: People with many influential relationships are almost always good to have on your side. They can help you find the right solution quickly and they often hear fresh news before everyone else does. People with strong connections are seldom out of work, and if they are, it's not for very long. More likely, they are the first ones to get tapped to go to a new employer.

On The Move: Some people seem to stay in the same place for a long time and others are always going somewhere new. People that move frequently are usually part of the power base in the organization and have the kind of broad political support that brings job security. You can advance your career just by following in their footsteps.

Apolitical: Office politics are an inevitable force in the white-collar workplace. Ignore them and you may become their next victim. Your goal should be to keep a safe distance from any kind of gamesmanship. The trick is to connect with people who understand what's really going on behind the scenes and know who's on whose side. Talented people who remain safely apolitical get promoted while those around them are fighting like cats and dogs.

Experienced: It's impossible to possess the first three traits unless you've been around for a while. Time on the job is often not enough; it's the depth of engagement and variety of assignments that enable someone to be exceptionally experienced.

Broadly Appreciated: You can learn a lot about someone from the diversity of the people who hold him or her in high esteem. People who are well regarded by both executives and mail clerks tend to be sincerely good people.

Of course, there is a corollary set of traits that can tip you to the fact that someone should be avoided. Beware of people who gossip about others, complain about the company and management, work in relative isolation, and seem to have been in the same job too long. Hanging around them too much can immediately damage your career before you know it.

Getting On The Radar Screen

Although you can get away with a lot of ignorance and very little contribution for the first month or so, it won't last long. Once your time has passed as the new guy, you better start scoring points or your new career may quickly stagnate. All of those nice people you met during your incubation period are going to remember you as a newbie until you dramatically show them otherwise. Once you've learned enough to contribute, you have to start building your reputation. Remember, the company was running along just fine before you arrived and someone else was doing everything that was important. This means what you do at first will be unimportant unless you get on the right people's radar screens.

The Big Boss

Unless you went to work for a psychopath, the person who hired you is going to be on your side for at least a year and keenly aware of how much you're contributing to the company. The same cannot be said for his or her boss. In fact, it may be just the opposite. In a number of jobs I've had, I've discovered after the fact that the Big Boss never believed that I was a necessary hire, and he reluctantly approved my position simply to appease my supervisor. Until I finally proved myself to him, I was little more than an expensive annoyance.

I ran into this problem during my first job after college. The man who hired me seemed alright, but as it turned out he didn't care for his boss and the feeling was mutual. I had been hired to help implement an inventory control system. After a few weeks, I discovered that none of the executives in my department wanted the new system—it had been forced down their throats by finance. That made me highly irrelevant.

About three months into the assignment, the company froze overtime in an effort to control expenses. I happened to overhear an argument between the Big Boss and the Plant Manager and figured out that the department was going to be severely hurt by this new policy. When the time was right, I approached the Big Boss and offered to work on the factory floor after hours to help the plant catch up without taking any overtime pay. I figured I could do a little blue-collar work without damaging my white-collar reputation if no one was around to see it. I jumped from a mere nobody to future leader status in one night. Within a month, another manager who worked for the Big Boss approached me about a promotion. These events were not unrelated.

Later in my career, I moved to Prime Computer as a Marketing Strategist. It was during a time when the senior ranks of the company were turning over from the old ex-Honeywell gang to new management from IBM. The managers of the department that hired me were in over their heads and struggling to launch a new program to sell products through a network of authorized distributors. They talked a good game and carried a slide show with them wherever they went. Unfortunately for them, the new executives were not going to sit though their slide show, nor give them much time to verbally explain the program. Observing this, I took it upon myself to write a formal business plan that encompassed everything they were saying in a single document. I also taught myself to use a financial modeling tool and built a financial plan for the program. Since this was the only document that existed for the new program, it was an instant hit. And since I wrote it, I put my name and phone number on every page. Within a few weeks, senior executives were calling and asking me to explain details from the plan. Twelve months later, the guys who hired me were gone and I was running the entire program.

It's clear that both of these moves got me on the right radar screens early in new assignments and paid off big time. Although they could have backfired if my hiring manager saw them as an end-run of his authority. These moves succeeded because they were fundamentally good for the department and were tasks my bosses didn't want to do themselves. Here's the key: The best way to become

62

visible to your boss's boss without threatening your boss is to find an important job he doesn't want to do and do it well.

The Big Picture—Outside Your Department

Too many people limit their search for potential promotions to the department hierarchy they fall under. By that I mean they see their next career step as either replacing the boss or getting their boss's job in another company. This is the classic definition of a promotion, but unless you're in a very fast moving company, it may take decades to achieve. It has been my experience that moves that cut across departmental lines are easier to make, more rewarding, and ultimately improve opportunities for a promotion down the road. Executives like to promote well-rounded individuals with a broader perspective. Individuals who move horizontally across the company are often better connected and able to solve problems at lower levels in the organization. Also, since people that move around are more versatile, they are more likely to find a home during a layoff than a one-dimensional person who has never worked outside their original department. Building interpersonal bridges across departments is an excellent source of job security.

Before you can build these bridges, you need to get on their radar screen. As I indicated earlier, the people who serve you aren't going to do much for your career. Be nice to them, always put yourself in their shoes, and thank them generously for their efforts. On the other hand, I believe the real action is with the people you serve. They depend on you and the other people in your department more than you know. They notice everything you do well and never forget anything you do wrong. They are likely to have access to the people above you and aren't shy about telling tales. I believe these relationships are more critical to your career than those within your department.

After about a year into my first manufacturing job at Data Terminal Systems, I became one of the key people that the Sales Department went to when they needed a critical order. I was always responsive and did my best to come up with creative ways to solve a customer problem. One day I noticed that there was a supervisor's job open in Sales Administration and I applied for it. My background did not fit the requirements, but thanks to my reputation for coming through for the Vice President of Sales, I landed my first big promotion and stepped over a number of people in the Sales Department.

About ten years later I got chased out of Prime and landed a job as a "corporate account manager" at Computervision. This was essentially an overlay sales support job based in the home office. I coordinated sales strategies across multiple salespeople and customer divisions.

One of my accounts was Hughes Aircraft. The local sales representative in Santa Monica was a tough young woman named Karen Scott. I spent months trying to get Karen to collaborate with me on account strategy, but she just kept giving me lip service. One day when she was lamenting about how she was unable to go on a two-week vacation because Hughes was so demanding, I volunteered to stay in Los Angeles for two weeks and cover Hughes while she went away. She loved the idea and took the full two weeks. Serendipity struck and while she was gone a major sales opportunity surfaced at Hughes. I didn't tell a soul. I waited for her to get back, and let her take all the credit for finding the deal. She became a good friend and a supporter. Her management knew that she was a tough nut to crack and once I earned her trust, they suddenly gave me a lot more respect. Six months later, I was offered the District Manager position for the Northwest United States. Again, these events were obviously related.

The Power Of Outside Resources

Up until now, I've been talking about ways to get on the radar screen through your own devices. This is very important for young people starting out in their career and helpful for everyone, but there is another way to get on the radar screen that is mostly applicable to workers with a few years under their belt: leverage relationships with outside vendors or service providers to build your reputation in a hurry. In the old days, most white-collar work was done within the four walls of the company. If you needed to do something new, you made the case to hire people to do it. This has all changed in the last decade through outsourcing. Today, companies expect employees to leverage outside resources to initiate new programs or provide specialized services on a time-critical basis. In many cases, these outside vendors have more expertise in their domain than anyone inside your company. By cultivating relationships with key outside vendors or service providers, you can instantly deliver incremental capabilities to your new job and get on the radar screen fast.

About 25 years ago, I worked with a fellow named John Shea. He was a very talented guy, and a jack-of-all-trades. He had been a competitive analyst, marketing program manager, and assistant to the Vice President of Sales. In 1987, he took over a telemarketing department that could no longer produce valid sales leads through in-house operators. Being a resourceful person, John started looking outside the company for help and discovered a company in Hampton Falls, New Hampshire that specialized in new forms of direct marketing. The company's founder, Tracy Emerick, had written books on the subject of direct marketing. Before spending a dime of the company's money, John and Tracy put together a killer proposal on how to radically improve lead generation at Prime and the project was approved. Not only did John score a major career success, but in the process he also became an expert in direct marketing. The last I saw of John, he had become Vice President of Marketing for a company that sold exclusively through direct marketing. I'm sure Tracy Emerick was there to help John during his first month on the job.

By making the most of the first 30 days and following it up with a solid initiative to get on all of the right radar screens, your new job is almost guaranteed to become a positive career move. The only other thing that can go wrong is to let minor job disappointments get blown out of proportion, develop a bad attitude, and damage your reputation before it's even established.

Temporary Discomforts

I may be a sucker, but for decades I always went into a new job anticipating that everything would be perfect. Of course, it never was. There were always surprises that came up and disappointed me. Over time, I've learned that they just go with the territory and generally go away before I know it. Of course, if you anticipate them and know that they're temporary, they will be a lot easier to take.

Boredom

Unless you're a little brain dead, no one likes to be bored. It closes in on you fast, particularly if it strikes at 10:00 a.m., and you've got nothing on the agenda for the day except lunch. The fact is, unless you have work to do, sitting at a desk is quite boring and new jobs are even worse. You can only create so many fact-finding meetings before they all run together and people get sick of talking to you.

The first trick to beating the boredom is to anticipate that it will occur and don't let it get you down. Remember, after about a month on the job you'll be reminiscing about the days when you had all that free time. Second, never let anyone know that you're bored. Managers want people with initiative and that means people who find useful things to do on their own. The last trick to fighting new job boredom is to actively seek out and embrace all work opportunities, even if they're beneath you. Most people are afraid to do menial tasks for fear of getting stereotyped as unworthy of their pay grade. My experience is that as long as you make it crystal clear that you're taking it on as a learning experience and because you have some temporary free time, people never hold it against you down the road. Instead, you earn a reputation right out of the gate as a team player that is confident in his or her place in the world. More often than not, the person

66

you reach out to help will be a friend for life and your boredom will end!

Projects You Don't Understand

I had one boss who called me into his office on the first day and gave me a half a dozen projects to work on immediately. This was my third job as Marketing Vice President and I knew the territory pretty well. The assignments he handed me required deep knowledge of the market, customers, and products. I had no idea what he was talking about or where to begin. Rather than argue with him, I listened intently, took notes, and left with the projects in hand.

Within the next 24 hours, I made lists of information I would need to know in order to get started on each project. On the third day, I met with my boss again and went over the lists of necessary information. He told me what he knew off the top of his head and then gave me names of people to see to get the rest. I doubt that I ever completed any of those projects, but two good things came out of the exercise. First, I got to demonstrate critical thinking skills to my boss; and second, I learned a lot about how things got done and who to go to for important information. None of this would have happened if I had protested an obviously unfair assignment that first day.

Office Space

When my daughter got her first marketing internship, she called me and, among other things, told me about her office space: "Dad, they stuck me at the desk right by the front door." Even at this young age, she figured out that she had won the rookie prize of the worst space in the office. No one wants the desk by the front door. You're constantly interrupted, everyone watches what you're doing, and it's impossible to have a private phone conversation. But she was both the new kid on the block and the most junior, so that's the seat she got.

One of the biggest mistakes I made in my early years was to place far too much significance on the quality of my assigned office space. If I thought that my space was at all below that of my peers, I'd beat a path to the boss and start whining. The truth is office space assignments are almost never fair; they can't be. Space is assigned on a first come, first served basis, so the new guy always gets the leftovers. If that's you, just suck it up and get used to it. Complaining is a sure way to signal to your boss that you're a self-centered, non-team player, with warped priorities. Relax. In most cases you'll only be stuck in substandard space until somebody leaves or the time comes to move to new space. That is the only time when office space allocation is perfectly fair. Accepting poor office space with grace is a way to demonstrate that you're a big picture person and a team player.

A few times in my executive years, I tried to buck the trend and carved out superior space for a promising new hire; it always backfired. The rest of my team immediately assumed that the new guy was destined to become their next boss and shunned him. Life would have been much easier if I had just stuck him in a small cubical by the front door.

Indifferent Support

Most white-collar workers have a team of support people who take care of the mundane details of work life like distributing reports, booking travel, scheduling meetings, getting overnight deliveries to the mailbox on time, etc. These folks are typically punching a clock and making peanuts. They are also often masters of their own domain. They decide whose work gets done first and what gets shoved to the bottom of the pile. The boss always comes first, but after that they play favorites. People who are nice to them, bring them cookies, or just treat them like human beings get timely support. New guys who look like they think they're important get squat. Unlike the other minor disappointments you'll encounter on your new job, this is one you can do something about from the very beginning. I always make a point of introducing myself to the receptionist, mailroom staff, and even the people in the cafeteria. In particular, I always go out of my way to make friends with the boss's secretary. Not only will this help you get things done, but your coworkers will also notice that the little people all know your name and say "hi" every time you walk by. This is very good for your reputation.

The Real Pay Policy

I haven't always gotten the shaft when it comes to office space or administrative support on a new job, but I can state unequivocally that I'm always disappointed when I learn how the compensation plan truly operates. Strategy Seven of *Career Secret Sauce* is devoted to salary policy and promotions, so I will just touch on two of the typical issues for now.

One thing you'll never hear someone say during the interview is "we've maxed out the pay grade to make you this offer and you won't see a decent raise unless you get promoted." But this happens a lot. Pay grades are like rearview mirrors: they reflect what the company paid people in the past for a given job. They never reflect the current market or the price people are willing to pay for a hot candidate in a field that's in high demand. Pay scales are set by the human resources department and are meant to be fair to all, not necessarily the best deal for a top ranked new hire.

The other thing you'll never hear during the interview is: "virtually no one ever gets 100 percent of their bonus." Yet, it's almost always true. You may have a letter in your hand that says you're being offered $75,000 a year; made up of $55,000 in salary and $20,000 in bonus, but in most cases the bonus pools are only funded at 80-90 percent of full payout. The rationale for this is that more people will fail to meet their objectives, than surpass them. The people who fail will get less than a 50 percent payout and those who go beyond will get over 100 percent. The problem is most managers are cowards and they're afraid to give someone a 50 percent payout. Invariably, payouts converge around the mean. If the mean is 85 percent, a superstar gets 95 percent and a laggard gets 75 percent.

You can either ask these questions after you get a written offer or not. It's certainly a good thing to know, but questions like these could scare off a potential employer or brand you as someone who is obsessed with money. If you don't want to ask, or you're already in a job and suspect these factors are negatively impacting your earnings potential, don't start complaining or take it personal. Just let it go and the next time you change jobs, ask the right questions and proceed with caution.

Just Develop *Thick Skin*

Your first new job is the most important one of your career, so it's important to make it go as smoothly as possible. Above all else, you need to get 2-3 years of experience under your belt before you can even think about making waves. Most workers will change employers a half a dozen times over the course of their career. The first one is critical, but any job change that goes poorly can set you back for years. It's incumbent upon you to make them all successful. Focus on what you can do to make your first job a success and the odds are excellent that you'll never make a bad move.

STRATEGY FOUR

Craft Your Winning Reputation

I'm not much of joke teller, but there is one tale that is so applicable to a variety of real world on-the-job situations that I've told it dozens of times—occasionally to the same audience.

It's the story about Pat and Mike.

Pat and Mike were on a camping trip and suddenly there was a loud noise and growl coming from the underbrush. Pat screamed, "What's that?"

Mike replied, "I think it's a grizzly bear" and with that Pat grabs his running shoes and starts lacing up.

"What are you doing Pat?" Asked Mike. "You can't outrun a grizzly bear".

"I know," said Pat "I don't have to outrun the grizzly; I just have to outrun you!"

The reason I think this joke is so applicable is because organizations (the grizzly) constantly compare employees (Pat and Mike) against one another to decide who is more worthy for key assignments, bonus pool shares, raises, and promotions. You don't have to be the best in the world, or even within your industry; you just have to be

71

"better than Mike" or whoever else your boss or organization is comparing you to.

Although most companies hire a fair amount of senior people from the outside, they do so reluctantly. They know that the odds of success are against them, and nothing is worse than passing up an internal candidate for a promotion in favor of an outsider who crashes and burns within the first year. This fear means that the preferred pool for virtually every plum job defaults to the current crop of employees.

In a perfect world, managers would make these critical personal decisions based exclusively on the work product of individuals involved. It would be a pure meritocracy. In our imperfect world, these decisions are never made on work products alone; in fact, too often actual person's work product has little to do with who ends up on top. These decisions are frequently based on the candidate's reputation; which is often a reflection of their visible work habits. People who are perceived as having great work habits move up and those who don't languish, hoping to avoid a layoff. For this reason, the fourth strategy in *Career Secret Sauce* is about how to Craft Your Winning Reputation.

A Necessary Desperate Measure

I detest acts of desperation. They signal a spiritual surrender on behalf of the actor and seldom achieve success. My rule of thumb for a successful career is to steer clear of any kind of desperate measures and to find another way out.

The exception to this rule is your reputation. It is pretty much all you have and you must defend it at all times, no matter how desperate it seems. If you can create a reputation for strong work habits, it will protect you from a multitude of career threats you never saw coming. On the other hand, a reputation for poor work habits is the ultimate "Scarlet Letter" for a white-collar worker. Once it's been pinned on you, it is virtually impossible to remove. It will even follow you from employer to employer; you simply can't let this happen to you. Clearly, there are some people in the workplace who are just plain lazy. They're welcome to read this book, but I don't think it will do them a lot of good. All of the meticulous image management efforts in the world will not save a genuinely lazy person; their true colors will emerge and nothing can protect them. Far too often, though, honest, hardworking employees inadvertently damage their reputation or miss opportunities to craft a stronger one because they simply didn't know any better.

Your work ethic is a classic intangible attribute. You can't see it, weigh it, or measure it, yet somehow people develop perceptions about who has a good one and who doesn't. Unfortunately these perceptions get cast early in your career and are very tough to change once the die is cast.

The key is to understand how and when perceptions about your work habits get formed and then consciously manage your behavior to shape the reputation you want and deserve. Above all else, steer well clear of any behavior that might earn you the scarlet letter of a weak work habit.

Don't Waste Your Youth Being A Youngster

Career Secret Sauce is all about creating a great career and still having time for a personal life. The personal life it seeks to preserve is the one that gets threatened during the child rearing years. That's when the tug-of-war between career and family gets intense. In your early working years, carving out spare time is just not very important. In the autumn years, the "empty nest syndrome" takes over and people often find themselves looking for something to do with all of their newfound free time. But for people in the middle of their working lives, who are busy raising a family, this time is often irrationally precious. These are the years of ballet recitals, after school birthday parties, school plays, softball games, and family dinner every night (at a reasonable hour). A workaholic lifestyle generally threatens the family life, just when the success of one's career is at its greatest risk.

Organizations are pyramid shaped. There are plenty of new jobs around for people with 3-5 years of experience and little competition for advancement, but once you enter the management years, things tighten up. Of course, this is often the same point when your family starts to want you at home more often. There is no simple solution to this chronic dilemma, but if you enter these work years with a solid reputation for a good work ethic, the strain can be significantly reduced.

My first recommendation is to strategically invest much of your free time during the first five years of your career crafting the strongest reputation possible. This will enable you to build a "work ethic cushion" that will help you cruise safely through the family years, working a 40-hour week and missing few key family affairs. You will be working a lighter schedule during these years, but because of the reputation you earned as a dedicated worker in the beginning of your career, people will barely notice.

Of course, you could start your career like many young people by missing a lot of Fridays and Mondays due to late night parties, habitually rushing to your desk with a coffee and donut in hand at 9:05 a.m., or putting more time in as the captain of the company golf team than you do at your actual job. If you choose one of those routes, you can easily wind up in a "work ethic black hole" when your family arrives and they need you most.

The point is simple. When you're young, single, and have plenty of free time, don't squander it living the life you may have enjoyed in college—get serious. Invest your free time logging extra hours and building a reputation as a passionately dedicated worker. It's like putting money in the bank. So when the day comes that you have to choose between working late or the little league playoff game, you've built up enough "work ethic equity" to take off a little early and go to the game without worrying about your reputation.

Your Word Is Your Bond—Follow Through Is Everything

At the risk of oversimplifying life, it seems to me that there are two types of people in the world: those who are always on schedule and those who are never on schedule. If you are one of the former, your odds of earning a reputation for a great work ethic are very high, but if you're one of the latter, a big red light needs to go off in your head immediately. This is something you have to actively compensate for at work or your career will likely be a lifelong struggle.

By people who are always on schedule, I mean people who have a subconscious checklist of everything they promised to do for others and when they said they'd get it done. People like this never surprise their boss, coworkers, or even subordinates by missing a deadline. That doesn't mean they get everything done on time and doesn't mean that their work product is all that great—they just seem to respect other people's expectations more. In fact, most of the schedule-obsessive people I've worked with actually do less real work than others, but if they tell you on Monday they will "pick a pound of pickled peppers" by next Friday and they discover on Wednesday that they can't, they'll be in your office first thing Thursday morning with a back-up plan and a heart-felt apology.

People who are never on time have a very different approach. I remember a guy at XPORTA who had an uncanny knack for inserting himself into the critical path of everything that went on in the company. We encouraged him to do it because the quality of his work product was so high that we all wanted his help.

I once asked him to do a small project for me. After we agreed to the specification, I asked him when he'd have it done and he told me about all of the other things he was working on. I then asked him again and he told more about what he was already working on. In frustration I asked him if he could have it done by Monday and he said, "Sure, I can't see why not." Monday came and the project wasn't done. In fact, he hadn't even started on it. Something else came up that he deemed more important and he simply dropped my project. What was funny was that he felt no remorse for this failure to deliver. I did everything I could to confirm when the work would be done, but in his mind he had never actually agreed to get it done by Monday, he was answering a rhetorical question: "Can you see any reason why this can't be done by Monday?" At the time he couldn't think of any reason, so he said "yes." He never considered what he did as missing a deadline. He had simply rendered an opinion about a hypothetical timeline and nothing more. After he and I talked, something else came up that he deemed more important and that's why my project wasn't done by Monday. When I questioned him for missing the deadline, he told me his rationale and felt fully vindicated for failing to deliver.

Several times I tried to explain to him that this behavior was severely damaging his career, but it was like talking to a brick wall. He sincerely believed that his responsibility was simply to do the best he could on the projects he took on and try to do the most important things first. In his mind, it was not his job to manage other people's expectations of his output. As his executive, I had no choice but to start cutting him out of every important project he was working on. It wasn't that he had a bad work ethic; he simply had a warped one.

If this sounds familiar, dump a bucket of cold water on your head; you need to change your behavior right away! You cannot have a safe and prosperous career if you underestimate the importance of follow-through. But, if you have this ailment, do not despair; I have a cure for you. It's called "The List" and it's the focus of Chapter 5.

Profile Jeff Morrill
Developing Your Greatest Asset; Your Reputation

Jeff Morrill has always been driven. He was a passionate football player and an explosive mogul skier. Although he grew up in the small rural town of Burnt Hills, New York, he pushed for big things at a young age. Jeff loved his family, but just had to get out of the house and start on his life as fast as possible. He had a great job in high school and decided to use his income to pay for an apartment. Jeff moved out and started living on his own at the tender age of 16 and maintained an A average in school.

He went from Burt Hills to Lafayette College. He played football and joined a major fraternity. Eventually, he became President of the Interfraternity Council. His big accomplish was to curb underage drinking at fraternities. This was clearly an unpopular initiative, but one that spoke volumes about Jeff and his commitment to personal responsibility.

Jeff got his first job at Nestle as a salesman. He was very aggressive and earned "Salesman of the Year" honors. He loved the sales lifestyle because he could work hard and then sneak off for a long ski weekend. He went from Nestle to Borden and his career in sales took off. As his responsibilities expanded, he got more involved in marketing and he liked it. Eventually, this led to his first big break in marketing at Johnson and Johnson.

Jeff has always been outspoken about the importance of a good reputation. Recently we met and he shared some of his thoughts with me as well as the events that shaped them.

Your Reputation is Everything
"A reputation is what people think of you; it is the naked truth about who others believe you are. Your reputation is uncensored, it's not something you talk about, it just lingers in the background of everything you do. It's also the ultimate personal attribute. The

way people treat you might reveal something about your reputation, but these clues are so subtle they're very difficult to detect. That's why I've always assumed that my reputation is very fragile and I "work" every day to enhance it; it's really who I am.

"Your reputation is your most precious asset and you should treat it like one! It's kind of like a bank account—you have to make regular deposits and build up the balance so it will be there when you need it on a rainy day."

Be Honest With Yourself and Others
"This is the start of building a reputation. Simply call a spade a spade. So many people beat around the bush or tell folks what they want to hear. This may win you points in the short run, but ultimately could damage your reputation. Sticking with the truth will never hurt your reputation."

Set Realistic Goals
"It's okay to be a little aggressive when it comes to setting goals, but they must always be attainable. I see a lot of people who try to be tough and come up with goals that are actually dreams. Before long, their credibility evaporates and no one trusts them. Be honest with your team, your boss and yourself about the goals you set. Invest time helping people understand your vision for success and what it will take to achieve it. This will foster alignment and win their support for the objective."

Consistently Exceed Your Commitments
"When you tell people you're going to do something and then you deliver, people remember. Make it a habit and your boss will start giving you all of the high profile assignments. This is one of the best reputations you can achieve. When something significant comes up, people think of you as one who can rise to the occasion."

Enroll Other People In Your Initiatives
"People love being associated with a winning effort. Get people involved in what you're trying to do and they'll jump on the band wagon to support you. As

things progress, share the glory and recognize the contributions of others. You can even win people over by simply keeping them in the loop about your initiatives. No one likes to be left in the dark. Recruit others, keep everyone informed, and you'll quickly earn the coveted reputation as a 'team player'".

Never Stop Enhancing Your Reputation
"In 2007, my reputation opened a new door for me at Vectrix. They are a much smaller dynamic company that is blazing a new market with the world's first 100 percent electric powered motorcycle that produces zero emissions. Someone that knew me from Johnson and Johnson introduced me to the CEO. We met to explore options and quickly I was offered the job of leading marketing for the Americas. From there I simply followed the lessons I learned at Johnson and Johnson to build the team, invest in people and the company. Within six months I was promoted to Chief Marketing Officer. The passion I have for developing the people around me has really paid off. It's also nice to get more responsibility and money by continuously investing in my reputation. But what really matters is what I see when I look in the mirror each day and ask myself—did I make a difference? Today I did."

The techniques that Jeff talked about will undoubtedly help you craft a winning reputation. These are solid tips that cannot only help you establish a solid career, but may even set you up for promotion. There are a few additional tips that I've discovered along the way that may not be as lofty as Jeff's, but will also help you to enhance your work ethic reputation.

Mix It Up (Your Work Hours That Is)

The first sign of a bad work ethic is showing up late and leaving early. Most people are smart enough to figure this out and avoid it whenever possible. The first cousin to this obviously dysfunctional behavior is showing up and leaving at the exact moment regular work hours begin and end.

Again, most people don't follow either of these problematic work habits. Instead, they may show up a little early, around 8:25 a.m., leave for home a little after 6:00 p.m., thus delivering a 48-hour work week, and establishing a reputation for having a very average work ethic. There is nothing wrong with this, but you are logging an extra eight hours a week and doing nothing to build your reputation.

My recommendation is mix up your starting and quitting time and avoid anything that looks like a regular pattern. This could mean coming in at 7:00 a.m. on some days and staying until 8:00 p.m. on others. You might even throw in an occasional Saturday morning or even a Sunday afternoon. Once you've developed this reputation, you can also come in at 10:30 a.m. now and then or leave directly after a late lunch and virtually no one will notice. Here's a tip: when you come in very early or stay very late, wander around to see who else is there. You'll see them and they'll see you. Can you hear the sound of your work ethic cash register ringing?

The reason this works so well is that normal workers never come in very early or work very late unless they're ordered to do so. When you start doing it once or twice a week, people quickly conclude that you have an extraordinary work ethic.

The Good, Bad, and the Ugly of Extracurricular Company Activities

What could possibly be more harmless than volunteering to run the company softball team? It gets you out of the office early a few nights a week, you get to mingle with your coworkers, and you even get to know a few ex-jock executives in an informal setting. Besides that, perhaps you're a good player and you can show off to everyone by hitting a home run or making a diving catch. Big mistake!

Volunteering to run an extracurricular team sport, particularly one you're good at, is the kiss of death for building a reputation for a good work ethic. First off, it
80

signals management that you'd rather leave work early and get to the field than stay in the office and work. If you're a better ball player than worker, they may conclude that you have your priorities mixed up. There is virtually no upside and a large downside to running an extracurricular company sports team.

What about just playing on the team and not running it? That could be good or bad, depending on your reputation. If you're a young jock, it will probably tarnish your image. If, on the other hand, you're a bit of an introvert, bookworm, or slightly over-the-hill and you play the game well, you may actually help yourself by creating an image as a multifaceted individual.

There are some extracurricular activities that can help you reputation. Charitable events are a good example. One year at Prime, Joe Henson, the President, was named the Chairman of the United Way for Massachusetts. This meant that he would be severely embarrassed if the per-employee donations at Prime were less than those of our competitors. I remember a lot of middle managers who jumpstarted their rise to power by signing on to help Joe raise money for the United Way. Of course, fundraising at work can be a double-edged sword. There were a lot of people who are offended by the idea of their employer soliciting donations on-the-job, particularly programs like the United Way that automatically dock a percentage right off your paycheck.

Writing an article about a new company strategy, department accomplishment, or new product for the company newsletter can also help your reputation. The idea is to write something that your boss would have written if he had more time. Of course, if you write an article about who won the egg toss at the company picnic, or who had the best costume at the Halloween party, it's kind of like the softball team effect.

One of the best extracurricular things you can do is to provide hospitality to out-of-town business guests.

Visiting customers are the best, but employees from across the country or around the world are almost as good. When you volunteer to show them the town, come to your home for dinner, or stay with you, you begin building an image as a goodwill ambassador for the entire company. You make the company look like a better place to work or buy products, and senior executives absolutely love employees who serve others this way.

Separation Of Work And Family

There is a classic "career limiting" mistake that I see happening over and over again. People with marginal reputations cite the needs of their family as a reason for poor performance. It might be coming in late, leaving early, or a conflict with an offsite meeting or business trip. Almost everyone has a family of some sort and most people would rather be at home with them than at work. People who wear family commitment on their sleeve are in effect proclaiming that they care more about their family than other employees. They are also broadcasting to the world that they can no longer balance their personal and professional time. Once the family becomes an excuse for not being able to participate in a company activity or get a job done on time, the employee's prospects for promotion vanish.

Therefore, I urge you to think twice, before you trot out a family conflict as your excuse for missing anything at work. This doesn't mean that you can't mention your family at work. In fact, suppose you had a meeting that ran until 7:00 p.m. and thus you missed the first half of your daughter's basketball game. There is nothing wrong with telling your boss the next day "I'm sure glad we got that meeting wrapped up by 7:00. I was able to catch the last half of Natalie's game and I saw her sink two free throws to clinch the win." Then your boss knows you have a personal life that you care about, but that you don't let it interfere with getting your job done. Next time, he may even check with you before unilaterally usurping your personal time!

Train 'Em To Trust You At Home

The ultimate prize in the work ethic sweepstakes is to earn a reputation that is so strong that no one ever questions what you're doing when you work at home. Your goal should be to achieve this trusted position before you enter the child rearing years, so that when junior comes along, you already have the means to spend more time at home without expending an ounce of career capital.

How do you achieve this coveted privilege? You earn it. Here is a simple formula that almost guarantees you'll be trusted to work at home in 6 months.

1. **Demonstrate Enhanced Productivity at Home**— Managers are suckers for ideas that improve productivity; it's the only way to get more work done when resources are limited and resources are always limited. Show your boss that you're more productive at home and she will welcome your plans to work out of the house. In the beginning, this is a catch-22. It's hard to demonstrate you're more productive at home without first working at home! My recommendation is to demonstrate your productivity first by doing so on your own time. One Friday afternoon, announce to your boss that you're going to try and tackle a particularly difficult project the following week. Then work on it over the weekend and deliver it to your boss first thing Monday morning. As your boss showers you with praise, point out that it was only possible because you're more productive working at home.

2. **Be Accessible at Home**—Managers fear allowing people to work at home because they're afraid that they aren't actually working when they can't see what they're doing. This is the beauty of email, cell phones, and Blackberries. If you can create an image of "always accessible" at home, your boss will be much more comfortable letting you work out of the house. Start by writing or answering emails from home very early in the morning and late at night. Make phone calls to your

boss's office phone on weekends and leave messages. By all means, respond quickly to emails or phone calls that come in outside working hours.

3. **Put it All Together**—Once you've set the stage with the two steps listed above, all you have to do is wait until the right opportunity presents itself and you can establish work-at-home privileges. What is the right opportunity? First, it's when the boss needs to get something really big done in a limited amount of time. Second, you have to know beyond a shadow of a doubt that you can get it done on time if you work at home. Most importantly, make sure you deliver. Once you nail one big project this way, the path is clear to making working at home a regular part of your schedule. Don't overdo it, but make sure that you exercise this privilege every month or so. Otherwise the boss may forget just how productive you are at home.

Make Email Your Best Friend

Even if you can't mix up your hours or convince your boss that you're more productive at home, there is one thing that everyone can do that will enhance their work ethic reputation: stay online nights and weekends. Do whatever you have to do to enable yourself to get work emails at home. Check emails regularly and respond quickly, especially late at night or on weekends. The response doesn't have to be complete or even well thought-out. A response as simple as, "good point, let me think about it and get back to you," signals that you're engaged in the welfare of the company at all hours of the day and night. Contrast that to someone who responds to an email that was sent out at 4:45 on Friday afternoon at 9:30 on Monday morning. What does that say about that person's work ethic? It may not be fair, but it's a fact that people equate responsiveness with a strong work ethic. Responsiveness is the easiest way to build work ethic equity.

Then There's Always "The Doctor's Appointment"

I said earlier that this entire chapter was one big desperate measure. Before we move on to Strategy Five and my time management techniques, I want to leave you with the ultimate desperate measure for getting out of the office unscathed. This technique is only effective when used judiciously, so be careful. Personally, the only time I ever used it was for when I was interviewing for a new job or some super critical family event. It works like this: When you just have to get out of the office and nothing else will do, put a "Dr." prefix in front of the name of the person you're meeting on your calendar. This works particularly well with group or departmental shared calendar programs. Trust me, no one is going to ask you why you're seeing a doctor and whether or not it can be moved. Obviously, there is some deception involved in this desperate measure, but sometimes you just have to clear your calendar and a vacation day isn't a viable option.

Remember, This One is All Defense—It's Not About Offense

Your reputation will never get you a big raise or a nice promotion on its own. You'll have to earn those things through the quality of your work product and the way you interact with others. This strategy really doesn't help you get ahead; it simply helps you avoid being stuck behind everyone else, just like Mike and the Grizzly. It is far more vital to craft a winning reputation in the first 10 years of your career than the last 25. In fact, those of you with more than 10 years of experience may have already learned some of these lessons the hard way, hopefully before any serious damage was done to your career. Steer clear of the pitfalls that can tarnish your work ethic and you'll find yourself well positioned to apply other strategies of *Career Secret Sauce* to move ahead. More importantly, you'll find yourself with the ability to create free time and still have a personal life!

STRATEGY FIVE

Do What You Say You'll Do

In school, doing what you said you'd do was somewhat optional. If you stiffed your parents, you may have gotten punished, but since they love you, it wasn't too severe. Teachers may have been a little tougher, but ultimately it came down to a grade and there was always extra credit work. Now you're playing for keeps. Drop the ball for the wrong person and you're in serious trouble. Not only can it kill you in your current job, it may follow you after you leave. That's why I invented "The List" as a tool for managing your time in the most effective manner.

To a certain extent, *Career Secret Sauce* is all about time; specifically your precious time, where you spend it, and what you spend it on. You want control of your time and to be able to physically get away from work when you want to for personal reasons. More importantly, your long-term well-being depends on your ability to get away from work mentally when you need to; you can slowly go crazy if you bring work home with you every night.

As you start your new career you may think that the best way to get ahead is to devote every waking minute to your new job. Of course, this would decimate your social life, but people would probably take notice and it might help you climb the corporate ladder a little faster. But if working eighteen hours a day guaranteed a successful career, more people would do it and no one in management would ever have a personal life. We know this is not true. There are plenty of knuckleheads who work like dogs 24/7 and never get past the ranks of supervisor or foreman. On the other hand, many executives have great personal lives; they spend quality time with their kids, play golf quite well, volunteer for charitable fund-raisers, and even write books.

The amount of personal time that you hand over to your employer is not the only factor determining the success of your career; in fact it isn't even the most important. The most important factor is how well you use your time on the job, the amount of work you produce in a given time period, and the quality of your work. Your ability to consistently get things done on schedule means a lot more for your career than the number of hours you clock, but even this means little if you're not doing the right things and doing them in the proper order. How you set your priorities and balance your efforts across competing demands is also critical to your job security. You must regularly feed the wolves to keep from getting eaten alive.

More Than Time Management

Like most white-collar workers, I've had my share of time management. I've read the books, worked the Daytimers and the PDA's (Personal Data Assistants), and sat through my share of all-day workshops on some proven time management technique.

Every time management system has the same basic components:

- Capture every potential task in a persistent format.

- Review the "to-do" list regularly to make sure you do "first things first".

- Establish a process for systematically protecting your-self from distractions.

- Use some clever tool (a book, software application, or device) to manage things.

I have no argument with any of these things (except perhaps the last one—I found that a blank bound notebook was the best persistent format). Invariably, the overhead associated with following the rules for using any of these off-the-shelf tools eventually crushed their effectiveness. I detest these expert time management techniques because they fail to help with the most critical element of time management. They do nothing to help me to figure out what to do first and ultimately, that's all that matters.

"The List" is more than a time management system; it's a way of critically thinking about how to invest your time at work to optimize your career success. It does this by helping you to systematically select the right set of priorities then focus on them when you're most productive. It forces you to reverse engineer the successes that will build a great career and helps you achieve them day-by-day.

You Can't Count On Your Boss

One trap a lot of new employees fall into is to assume that their boss will tell them what to do and when to do it; therefore, they don't have to set their own priorities. I have to admit that I've fallen into this pit a few times when I was under an oppressive workload or facing a critical deadline, but it always turned into a disaster. There are a lot of reasons why blind obedience always fails, but here are a few of my favorites:

1. **You Put Your "Personal Franchise" at Risk:** A job that builds a career is more than the endless stream of assignments handed to you by your boss, it's the functional role in an organization that you've been assigned to fill: I call it your "personal franchise." Your job title stakes out your turf, but that's all. Your reputation is built on your ability to define and negotiate lofty goals, set bold strategies, and deliver results that exceed the expectations. If you do this with

creativity and passion, people will take notice and your career will move ahead. On the other hand, if you ignore your franchise and just mindlessly process tasks that come your way on a first-come first-served basis, others will pass you by. Some bosses understand the importance of helping subordinates build their "personal franchise" and will mentor you in this endeavor. Others are selfish and only see you as tool to help them build their own place in the organization. They expect you to dedicate yourself to their success and promise to take care of you when the time comes. At the bottom of the ladder, this may be okay, but as your career develops and you take on more defined roles, your ability to stake out a franchise and find the time you need to deliver on it is a huge career builder.

2. **People Will Just Go Around You:** Even in the very short run, you can't just tell people "I can't help you, I'm busy working on something critical," and have them actually disappear. Most often, they just go over your head, and ask your boss for the same thing; and most likely, the boss will pick up the phone and ask you to do it anyway. Of course, now you look like one of the little people and you've trained a peer to go to your boss to get you to do something whenever you say "no". It could be even worse. Perhaps the boss realizes that you turned away the coworker because you were working on his mundane list of tasks and he then asks another subordinate to do the job you should have done. If that happens, you just lost a piece of your franchise. In the long run, this cycle will conspire to keep you from ever earning the reputation you need to get promoted.

3. **It's a Cry of Surrender:** No matter how dedicated and talented you are, as soon as you start telling people to go away, you're sending out a signal that you're over your head and are incapable of taking on more responsibility. Another career kiss-of-death.

4. **R-E-S-P-E-C-T:** The fact is no one with any career aspirations will ever submit themselves to becoming their boss' personal slave. Witness the workplace, which has plenty of derogatory nicknames for people who choose submission; yes-man, kiss-up, brown-nose, etc. Anyone who accepts this role is sending a signal to their boss and everyone else in the organization that they have no self-respect. The more you blindly process work from the boss, the more work you'll be asked to process blindly!

The only asset you have for building a great career is your time. If you fall into the trap of giving it all to your boss, he may end up with a great career, but you probably will not. Yes, you must find a way to do what your boss asks you to do, but also have to "manage him" to enable you to find time to devote to the other competing interests vying for your time. All of these interests are vital for building a great career and "The List" is the tool you need to make it happen.

Your Competing Interests

Your "personal franchise", subordinates, coworkers, your boss' boss, his peers, and your boss all linger waiting to help or hurt your career. The priority you place on the projects they propose will either win them over or earn their animosity.

"The List" provides a way of systematically capturing the requirements dictated by these competing interests and then paying them off regularly to win their support for your career.

I've just touched on the pitfalls of blindly devoting yourself to your boss whims and workload, as well as failing to respond to coworker demands. While this can hurt your career, it is seldom fatal. Careers are often mortally wounded when you get caught in the political crossfire that occurs between your boss and his or her peers. If you can train your antennae to detect threatening situations and handle them with grace, you will earn your boss' trust and respect. Blindly stumble into one of these high-octane political skirmishes, and your boss may just throw you under the bus and sacrifice you to save his own skin.

The Mind Game Of Politics

I've spoken to a number of white-collar workers with operational responsibilities about what happens to them on Sunday nights. They say that's when the sense of impending doom sets in regarding Monday morning. That's because Monday morning is the time when most businesses hold operational reviews to checkup on the people who are responsible for producing sales numbers, meeting forecasts, etc. Reviews like this are particularly daunting because you often find yourself reporting to not only your boss, but his or her boss and many of their peers. If you're one of those lucky individuals being reviewed, it may feel more like a group shake and bake than a mere checkup. Whether it hits you on Sunday nights or some other time of the week, the sense that your career will be threatened by an upcoming accountability review can often make you physically and mentally ill. Your weekend is only two days long and if you find work sneaking into Sundays, it will only be a matter of time before you find yourself in a state of constant anxiety or depression.

This gathering dismay is often rooted in a sense that you haven't done what you said you'd do at the last review and this time you're going to get caught, raked over the coals, and perhaps suffer irreparable career damage.

Having struggled through my share of Monday morning reviews, I can tell you that fear was definitely a factor in my angst, but so was frustration. The executive scrutiny (and torment) never seemed to be dished out fairly; some people were given a pass for poor performance and others persecuted mercilessly. As a victim of frequent torment, I decided to study the difference between the people who were given a pass and those who were constantly tortured. In a nutshell, those that regularly breezed through operational reviews ("breezers") studiously listened to the various requests and suggestions made by reviewing executives and then framed their report for the following week to incorporate these tidbits. Despite the flagrant nature of this obvious appeasement, senior managers continuously fell for it and went easy on the happy breezer.

The victims of torment did just the opposite. When an executive started to criticize their results and make suggestions for improvement, they got defensive and tried to explain why that idea wouldn't work. They'd dig themselves into a hole and if they picked the wrong big shot to tangle with, they'd end up in a life-or-death confrontation. Meanwhile, the breezers would graciously thank executives for their suggestions, ask follow-up questions (seeking to better understand the wisdom the executive was espousing), and almost always take out a pen and take notes. I am not suggesting that the breezers were mindless "yes men"; in fact they probably put more thought behind what they did than most of us. They simply appeared to graciously capture the input from the executive peanut gallery and then played it back a week later to win favor. That didn't mean that they always followed the advice they received.

I eventually adopted this approach for my operational review presentations and my time on the griddle became much more pleasant. I would still get beat up from time to time, but I knew that I could manage the situation and little harm would come my way. Most importantly, I could enjoy my Sunday nights once again.

It's All About Your "Personal Franchise"

By and large, white-collar workers who spend all day processing work handed down from their boss are the least likely to get promoted. The reason is simple; the only person who can possibly appreciate their work is their boss and he's not about to kill the golden goose by promoting his own personal work-processing machine. If he's a high flyer and he's moving up, he may bring you along with him, but my experience is that the people who get promoted are developers of people, and these folks never relegate subordinates to this type of situation.

People get promoted for two reasons: first there is a widespread recognition that they are the best candidate for the job, and second, their name comes immediately to mind when the hiring manager starts to think about potential candidates. This means that your promotability depends on your ability to get on the radar screen of your boss' boss, his peers, and your coworkers as a person who is not only ready to take on more responsibility, but at risk to leave the company if it doesn't happen soon. The best way to achieve this recognition is to define and promote your "personal franchise."

Virtually every white-collar job has a semi-meaningful title. Your "personal franchise" begins by defining your vision of the charter associated with your title and then staking out goals, objectives, and strategies for deliverables that will win over your career constituency.

Ultimately, the deliverables you select should be worthy of becoming a highlight on your résumé under the heading "accomplishments."

Here are a few examples from my résumé:

- Established an in-house PR function (terminated original PR agency). Within 90 days, editorial coverage more than doubled, as did the quality of coverage.

- Led team of 160 sales and marketing personnel on the floor at industry's largest tradeshow and earned the award for "The Most Promising Company of the Future" (30 days after announcing a $515 million loss—the largest loss in the history of our industry).

- Created company's Strategic User Interface Initiative, resulting in company-wide adoption of new state-of-art design style and collaborative design process across 100 percent of the product line.

None of these accomplishments were on the job description when I accepted the position. I simply discovered an opportunity to fix what was broken and began peddling it as my new personal initiative. Over time, my boss and the entire organization came to agree that these were important projects for the company and my name was associated with the leadership of these initiatives. People would continue to expect me to complete the mundane tasks that were traditionally associated with my job title, but they appreciated that these new initiatives took precedent and cut me plenty of slack if the old work wasn't being done quickly. Don't misunderstand; this was not an act of insubordination. In fact, once I explained these projects to my boss, he or she wholeheartedly supported them. On multiple occasions, these new initiatives were so compelling that I was funded to hire new subordinates to handle the less glamorous tasks that fell under my self-defined "personal franchise."

Your "Personal Franchise" And "The List"

The beauty of defining bold projects in your "personal franchise" is that they can then be used to get control of your time. Imagine your boss walking into your office with a new idea that you instantly determine is a complete waste of time. Rather than jump into a no-win argument about the validity of his idea, you simply grab your notebook ("The List"), ask him to elaborate, write down all the details of his idea, tell him you want to research it, and patiently wait until he leaves. He thinks you're going to jump right on his idea, but nothing could be further from the truth. You never actually said when you'd work on it, or even if you would do it at all. You can now leisurely contemplate an airtight case for why it's such a bad idea. Once you've framed your argument, jot it down on "The List" right under your notes from the discussion with your boss. If your boss asks you about his idea later, simply pull out "The list" and report back your research, asking him to help you to rank it against all of the other projects on "The List" In particular, highlight the high-profile projects that you've taken on under your "personal franchise." If he's at all rational, he'll instantly conclude that your high-profile projects rank higher than his lame brain idea. Never suggest that his idea is a bad one or propose that it be terminated, just make sure it stays out of the top 5 priorities on your list. This will assure a slow and painless death.

Look at the beauty of this technique. In exchange for 15 minutes of your time, you successfully anesthetized the little canker sore your boss tossed your way. From that point on, you never have to waste another minute thinking about it. Eventually, your boss will become mildly irritated that you keep reminding him of his weak idea. By the way, as soon as you sense any irritation, drop the item from future discussions. Move it to the dead idea file. Not only will your boss be impressed with your persistent follow through, he may think twice before walking into your office with a half-baked idea in the future.

Apply "The List" Generously

I first developed the technique described above in 1993 and used it with a number of very creative and demanding bosses for over a decade. It always worked. Once it became second nature, I started using it on everyone who brought me work—not just my boss. Coworkers, subordinates, your boss' boss and his peers constantly feed you with suggestions for projects you might undertake. Since they're not your direct boss, you can often ignore them without obvious personal peril, but why do it? Why not use it as an opportunity to win them over and promote your "personal franchise"? Once you've adopted the technique of questioning someone else's idea in a non-judgmental manner, writing down the details, and offering to do some research and get back to them, you can start to build your own personal fan club without breaking a sweat. Not only does this provide a vehicle for enabling you to spend your time where you want to, it also gives you a platform for constantly reminding everyone about your "personal franchise" and just how darn busy you are completing the top priorities associated with it.

The Importance Of Balanced Output

Once you've mastered the art of capturing all potential projects on "The List", you have successfully balanced your work inputs. Now you're ready to balance your output. The first step is to understand its various dimensions:

The Organizational Dimension: You clearly can't please all of the people all of the time, but that isn't an excuse to ignore organizational balance when you're deciding your work priorities. Obviously, you want to devote a great deal of time to work that comes from your boss or supports your "personal franchise." The work that comes from your boss' boss and his peers is important, but if you devote all of your time to servicing senior executives, you may end up with a reputation as an executive kiss-up. Your subordinates are like your children and they require adequate care and feeding. Ignore them at your peril. Numerous studies have found that subordinates who lack attention from their boss are unhappy and highly likely to leave their job. But like children, subordinates will suck up all of your time if you let them. The one group that I find often gets ignored are your peers and coworkers. After all, you are essentially competing for future bonuses, raises, and promotions; why should you help each other? The reason is simple: your peers and coworkers will always be the ultimate gatekeeper for organizational promotions. As we'll discuss in Strategy Seven, promotions seldom go to the person who has the greatest work product; most of the time they go to the person that the organization finds most palatable as a new boss. Listen to your coworkers suggestions, take on small projects for them from time to time, and you're likely to earn their trust and respect come promotion time.

The Time Dimension: Some people will only work on the most urgent assignments. They love a good crisis and flourish in jumping from one fire to another. Somehow they never get around to working on anything that takes a long time to complete or doesn't have anyone clamoring to get it done. Others are the big project people. They detest firefighting and steadfastly keep their eye on the big picture. They can go for months without delivering a thing while they work on a "big bang" deliverable. It is difficult to have a successful career if you have either of these warped profiles and virtually impossible to succeed in management. My advice is to always have two or three big "personal franchise" projects in process while making sure that you deliver something of value every single week. Ideally, you want to time the big deliverables to come out right before bonuses are calculated or annual raises are set. They can also be a big life saver if you have one queued up for delivery just before layoffs are announced or budgets are getting cut. Finally, you must never become so dedicated to your work plan that you cannot just drop everything to jump on a good old-fashioned crisis. White-collar workers who have the ability to jump into a firestorm without destroying their work plan are deemed to have capacity for greater responsibilities (i.e. promotable)!

Your Biorhythm Dimension: When I first heard of biorhythms, I thought it was just junk science. According to the experts, "the theory of biorhythms claims that one's life is affected by rhythmic biological cycles, and seeks to make predictions regarding these cycles and the personal ease of carrying out tasks related to the cycles." As my career matured, I noticed that some days were better suited than others for different types of work and today I believe the Theory of Biorhythms to be profoundly true. Perhaps it's the halo effect of a nice quiet weekend, but I find it very difficult to jump into intellectually demanding work the first thing on a Monday morning; my mind is just not yet back in the game. For this reason, I try and queue up my backlog of mundane work for Mondays. That way I know I'm doing something useful and it clears my plate for more fun things the rest of the week. Most importantly, I know I won't do serious damage to my career by tackling a complex assignment and messing it up when not at my best. This also means that I have to prepare extensively if someone else schedules me into a daunting assignment for a Monday morning. If this happens, I'll devote a lot of time on the Thursday and Friday before prepping and then bring a prep package home with me to review both Sunday and Monday mornings. I may still be a little off, but I know I'll perform.

By the same token, I know that I do my best writing on Tuesdays and give my best presentations later in the week. I prefer to tackle serious personnel matters on Fridays. Of course, this is just me; everyone's a little different. I'm probably bastardizing the underlying science of Biorhythms, but I do believe that we can enhance the quality of our work, and our working life, by tuning into our personal biorhythms and then scheduling ourselves to do the type of work we do best at the times that are best for us.

Putting It All Together—The Mechanics Of "The List"

Now that you have the rationale and mental framework for "The List", all that's left is to put it in action. It's easy to get started, and if you are one of those disciplined souls who is already using a time management system, I would simply modify it to support principles of "The List"

Step 1: Start Maintaining a Persistent List Immediately— I always used a bound hardcover notebook. It felt more substantial and after a while, people knew that they had gotten my attention when I opened the book and started writing. Spiral bound notebooks or PDA's certainly work just as well. Scraps of paper, little yellow stickies, or personal tape recorders do not. Your "List" is your working playbook and it must be able to hold up for months at a time. It must be convenient to carry with you at all times. Be sure to tape a business card to it so that you have a chance of getting it back if you accidentally leave it somewhere. Once you have it, just start using it. Begin with the date, time, and names of the people you're talking to. If you're using a paper-based tool, leave room after you capture a suggestion to jot down your research and subsequent thoughts, plans, and actions.

Step 2: Set Your Priorities—Your "List" has two vital functions. First, it's your day-to-day game plan; the to-do list for what you're working on right now. You should always have a clear view of the top 3-5 things you've committed to and when you plan to have them done. Second, it's your comprehensive repository for every single idea, suggestion, or proposed project anyone in the organization has ever asked you to consider. Keep them numbered, even if the numbers assigned after the first 10 are simply chronological. If your boss ever asks you what you're working on you can tell him the top 3-5 and then recite the rest of your list. Once you've rattled off 20 or 30 line items you can solicit his opinion on the ranking of your priorities and allow him to move a few things up or down. I have never found a boss who wants to get involved in re-sorting a list of 20 potential projects coming from a dozen different people. This is a great way to keep him off your back.

Step 3: Actively Manage Your "List"—Your "List" is a living document and it's the best tool you'll ever find for protecting your right to allocate your time the way you choose. You should periodically review every line item and the priorities you've assigned. I always had a soft copy of my list on my laptop and that made it easy to change priorities or add and delete line items. Once I set my new priorities, I'd print a copy and use a glue stick to paste it to a new page on my hardcover notebook. To be effective, you need to develop a habit of checking your list once or twice a week. I suggest you pick a regularly scheduled time and make it sacred. If your department holds weekly staff meetings, schedule time to manage your list about an hour before the meeting begins. Friday afternoons or Monday mornings are also effective.

Profile Joe Petro
Deciding What to Do Next and How to Do It Right

Joe Petro is an extremely practical man. When he wants something he simply figures out the quickest and easiest way to get it, then he executes relentlessly. Math and science came naturally to him, so that's what he focused on in school. While Joe has always looked for a job that he enjoys, he never lost sight of the fact that the only rational reason for working for someone else is to make money. When it came time to specialize in college, Joe looked around and saw that the highest paying jobs were those related to computers, so that's what he studied. When he graduated from school in New Hampshire, he went to work for EDS on the General Motors account in Saginaw, Michigan, the biggest and best paying computer services company in town.

I met Joe at a small software company in Cambridge, Massachusetts called ICAD. The company had developed a program to simulate mechanical design and engineering. It was a form of artificial intelligence—very heavy stuff. The biggest problem was writing "the rules" for mechanical design. Programmers had to be expert mechanical engineers and proficient in an artificial intelligence programming language called LISP. Joe had taught himself to become an expert in writing ICAD models. I assumed he was a complete computer geek and never gave it a second thought.

One day Joe tendered his resignation to go to a new start-up company. His boss couldn't talk him out of it, so the president of the company gave me permission to try and change his mind. We offered Joe the opportunity to manage a new department. He took the job and excelled at it. That's when I really learned about Joe and his ability to figure out what to do next and how to do it right.

It turned out that he wasn't actually a geek. He was the owner and driver of a race car team, and also owned a gourmet pizza restaurant; all in his spare time. He also loved to snowboard. Joe has an incredible capacity to juggle multiple disassociated tasks at once and do them all well.

I later recruited Joe to join me at Aspect Development, another software company in Silicon Valley. As his work became more political, his formula for success continued to evolve. Romesh Wadhwani was the CEO of Aspect Development and a true business visionary. He was one of the first executives to open an engineering center in Bangalore, India. When Joe was interviewing I told him about Romesh's vision and he said "I'll do anything as long as I don't have to go to India."

Joe did avoid India for a while, but he quickly looked around and realized that no one wanted to go to India—other than Romesh. He also discovered that Romesh was right. The company could hire 10 very talented engineers in India for the cost of one in Silicon Valley. The pure practicality of this struck a chord with Joe. He realized it was a career making opportunity and committed himself to doing it well. In less than a year, he went from avoiding India like the plague, to the company's lead executive for Indian operations. Joe was promoted to Vice President and had over 1000 employees in India reporting to him.

Today Joe is the Senior Vice President of Product Development at a major healthcare systems company called Eclipsys. He got the job in part due to his experience in creating engineering centers in India. He still races his cars and dreams of snowboarding all day long one day. It will probably be sooner rather than later.

I recently had lunch with Joe and recapped his evolution from geek to senior executive. His secret sauce was his ability to focus very clearly on the things that had to get done first, manage his time relentlessly, and navigate all of the political landmines along the way.

Here are a few of Joe's pearls of wisdom.

Time is Currency
"The old adage, 'if you have to do something, then you have to do it WELL' is a crock. There are some things not worth doing well—these things just need to get done. I have met many people throughout my career that work 15 hours a day but waste seven of them on stuff you could do in one hour if you just set your mind to it—these folks never end up with a great career."

Doing it My Way is Less Important than Getting it Done
"Doing whatever it takes to move the product, project, or program forward FASTER is all that's important. Spend less time arguing about your way or their way. Spend all your time talking to the best people and finding a better way. You will soon develop a reputation as someone who pushes hard and gets it done fast and everyone will want to work with you. Avoid people that want to argue that their way is the only way. They will not be around for long."

Don't Ever Come Off as the Smartest Guy in the Room
"Raw intelligence has nothing to do with being the best leader, the highest paid person, or the one with the best career trajectory. Most of the wildly successful people that you meet in your career are not the sharpest knives in the drawer. Learn to recognize the strongest leaders and give them whatever you can to help them succeed. Your own success will follow."

Learn to Love Salespeople
"Salespeople are often obnoxious, arrogant and appear lazy. It's easy to simply dismiss them as an irrelevant, self-serving nuisance. They are not. Salespeople pay your salary, grow the company, and live a very stressful life—so figure out how to work with them. They also worry about the same thing the CEO does—how to grow the company. Winning internal company battles at the cost of losing the

sales war will kill your company. Working in a company that is a true sales and marketing machine can help you retire early!"

The More Technical You Become, the Tougher it is to Explain Your Ideas

"Learning how to market your ideas and explain them in terms everyone understands is crucial to success. If you cannot explain your ideas you will be labeled as a propeller-head and be relegated to the back room. On the other hand, if you can demystify the complex, you will earn a reputation as a go-to person with business savvy and the technical know-how to back it up. If you figure out a way to talk to clients and executives in a way that 'they get,' your career will really take off."

Every Year There are a Few Defining Moments When You Must Perform

"If you can recognize these moments and 'knock the ball out of the park' you will break away from your peers and be recognized by everyone as a star. It doesn't matter how many hours you put in or how many 'i's you dot or 't's' you cross. NEVER allow failure or mediocrity in these moments. I have personally found that this is the most important lesson of my entire career."

Silence is Golden

"I remember once when I was seven years-old and shooting my mouth off about nothing, my Dad said 'Joe, if you do not know what you are talking about then shut up.' While others are trying to explain their misinformed ideas you can come off as the smartest and most reflective guy in the room by simply remaining silent. If I had a dime for every time someone's mouth outran their brain in a business meeting I could have retired at 30. You will be amazed how much you learn by listening and observing. When the boss says 'Joe—what do you think about this' and everyone in the room stops and turns to you, make sure your answer is a good one. If you do you'll really shine because the big mouths have already disqualified themselves with their off-the-top-of-their-head babble."

It's Your Time

Time is all you have to invest in your career. You must use it to your advantage or risk being left behind while others move up the organization. "The List" is the best way I've found for forcing myself to critically examine what to work on and why. Done properly, it will protect you from a variety of political landmines, maximize your potential bonuses and help you to effectively position yourself for promotion. Take my advice and make "The List" part of your life starting today.

STRATEGY SIX

Master The Art Of Presentation

Imagine being able to call your manager around nine in the morning and tell her that you won't be coming in for a few days because the office is just too much of a distraction and she agrees you should work at home. Can you conceive of your contribution being so critical to your department, and your company, that no one wants to mess with you; that the mere thought of your resignation actually makes everyone you work for nervous?

Wouldn't it be nice to have a glowing letter go to your supervisor from another department commending one of your recent performances and knowing that it is just one of many you'll be receiving this year? Suppose you could capture the undivided attention of key people who are critical to the success of your career for 30 minutes and have them actually just sit and listen intently to everything you say?

Now picture your boss evaluating your performance in light of all of this (deciding your bonus, your next raise, or potential promotion) or considering whom in the department to layoff when times get tough (it's certainly not going to be you). It's quite simple to achieve this revered status: make it your business to master the art of presentation. It's not as hard as you may think and it's the best way to propel your career above the crowd. That's why it's Strategy Six of Career Secret Sauce.

The One Assignment Your Boss May Fear

In Strategy Eight, we'll be looking at Career Saving Moves. In the meantime, I'll give you a little preview: The best source of job security is to succeed on important work that others avoid. Presenting is probably the most fertile field for the application of this advice. Most people don't merely want to avoid giving presentations; the thought of doing so can actually make them physically ill.

There is a widely cited study from the Sunday Times of London in October of 1973. They asked 3,000 Americans what their greatest fear was. The results? 41 percent said, "speaking in front of a group," while 19 percent said, "dying." I have personally seen people break out in a cold sweat, struck down by laryngitis, or simply freeze like a deer staring into a car's headlights at the thought of speaking in public. If you're looking for an assignment that no one else wants, look no further.

In 2001 and 2002, I worked with a very talented executive; I'll call him Scott. Scott had a tremendous vocabulary, was very articulate, and spoke interactively in a small group with the eloquence of a Clarence Darrow. However, change the scenario slightly and tell Scott that he's making a presentation to that small group and pure panic ensued.

The first time I observed this was at a conference of about 100 investors in New York City. Scott and I were on a panel and each of us was scheduled to give a ten-minute speech on our respective business units. Just before Scott got up to speak he turned to me and said, "If I freeze up there, please come up and save me." His hands were shaking and I could tell from the look in his eyes that he meant it.

A man consumed with this kind of terror will do anything to get as far away from the source of his fear as possible, and that's exactly what Scott did. Shortly after that day, there was reorganization and Scott was promoted. Then I noticed that the subordinates he was recruiting all had one thing in common: they were slick presenters. By the time the annual sales kick-off meeting came around in January, Scott was nowhere on the agenda; his subordinates gave all of his presentations. Most members of Scott's senior staff were quite talented in other ways, but regardless of their skills, Scott looked out most for those that handled his speaking assignments. Not only did these well-speaking underlings get Scott's political protection, but they also received a lot of opportunities to strut their stuff in front of high-level audiences that peers in other departments seldom spoke to.

Your Coworkers Have Stage Fright As Well

The phenomenon of people passing up great public speaking opportunities is not just limited to managers and subordinates; it also happens among competing co-workers.

In the late eighties at Prime Computer, I had two subordinates who were constantly vying for the next promotion (I'll call them Karl and Jane). Karl was a very intelligent man with a financial background and he'd spend hours doing research and writing papers to demonstrate his talents. But he hated giving speeches. He would mumble and just read his notes when forced to speak to a crowd. Jane might have been as smart as Karl, but she certainly didn't show it. She had a striking appearance and had a background in sales. There, she had learned how to give a presentation that made things sound better than they actually were. She also knew that her speaking talent was valued by senior management and regularly sought out opportunities to give presentations.

Jane was more than happy to pick up the engagements that Karl ducked. In fact, Karl would automatically suggest Jane make every speech he was asked to do. My bosses ended up seeing a lot more of Jane than they did Karl. Whenever I tried to give Karl a raise, they'd pick his work apart. On the other hand, they were constantly pushing me to give Jane more responsibilities and bigger bonuses.

109

This situation became a real problem for me. Karl's insight and analysis were critical to the team's performance, and Jane was just an on-call speaker. Yet Karl's career was fraught with insecurity and Jane simply cruised along working nine to five and picking up fat raises.

Once you commit to becoming a great speaker, you'll instantly discover countless opportunities to advance your career. Your boss and most of your coworkers will most likely see you in a new, more favorable light and even bring you speaking engagements you might not have otherwise discovered on your own.

Everyone Loves A Good Spokesman

Your newly developed speaking prowess will probably put you in high demand. Moreover, you may even earn the support, admiration, and outright affection of your supervisor and coworkers, particularly if you're talking about them. White-collar work is very political and just like in political campaigns; departments are constantly running for office. They are seeking more headcount, increased funding, better facilities, and of course, promotions for everyone. With a little fine-tuning, you can turn any presentation into a showcase for the people you work with and thus become their eternal hero.

In 1993 at Computervision, I inherited an unusual subordinate—we'll call him Paul. Although he had been with the company for years, his services were never appreciated. He had bounced from the Prime Division to the Computervision Division, from the marketing department to the services department, and from product manager to sales. That was where he found his Career Secret Sauce. The Services Department was having a tough time explaining their new strategy for selling a new family of service products. They were trying to create an image that went beyond simply fixing what was broken. Paul recognized this and volunteered to become the spokesman for the new service department strategy. What's more, he fashioned his presentations in such a way as to promote the hidden skills and capabilities of his department. Suddenly, Paul was flying all over the world, telling people how great the services department was, and even better, the new service products were selling.

This development marked the end of Paul's career malaise. I recruited him into the marketing department for North America and made him our pitch man for the hottest new products we were promoting. About a year into working for me, Paul resigned to pursue a better paying job. As soon as word got out, executives and salespeople bombarded me, demanding that I find a way to make him stay. Since money was what drew him away, there was a simple solution. I gave Paul a huge raise and he ended up staying. I even recruited him a few years later to join me in another company and once again be a traveling spokesman for our new product strategy.

Paul figured out that by becoming the spokesman for the service organization, he could enhance his job security, compensation, and personal freedom. Quite possibly, the same sort of success can come to you.

Making Presentations Is Just One Big Job Interview

When you're speaking to a group, you have the power to command their attention. People not only hear the words you say, but they also develop a lasting impression of your communication skills and an enhanced perception of your intellectual prowess. Speakers who can carry themselves well at the podium are generally viewed as larger than life. If the audience is impressed with what you say and how you say it, they'll remember you and may even become fans for life.

In the summer of 1993, I was the Senior Marketing Manager for Computervision's North American Operation. Things were not going well. The company was losing money and an upstart competitor was hitting North America the hardest. We had scheduled a big sales meeting in Fort Lauderdale, Florida to unveil a new formula for increasing sales. As the senior marketing executive for

North America, it was my assignment to define the formula, create most of the material and deliver 80 percent of the first day's presentations. This would be a daunting task, and I struggled for weeks to find a theme that would win over a tough audience of seasoned salespeople.

The biggest problem Computervision had was its complicated product line. The company had been around for decades and suffered from overlapping products built on old technology, and new products that didn't actually work yet. The Corporate Marketing Department made matters worse. Every product had a marketing manager whose career hung on the unit sales of their product line. This meant that they never admitted to any product weaknesses and whenever they compared their offering to the competition, they made it sound like only a fool would choose something else over Computervision. The sales force knew this wasn't true. They believed that they were losing deals for product reasons, not bad salesmanship; but the not-so-hidden agenda in Corporate Marketing was to blame North American Operations for the company's weak sales performance.

This is when my epiphany for the formula hit me. All I needed to do was to delineate the stronger products from the weaker ones, and then focus the sales force on selling the products that were winning head-to-head competitions in North America. I could also point out which products were "dogs" and steer them away from wasting their time pitching them. Poking fun at these hapless offerings would provide me with grist for making jokes at the expense of the home office—something the sales force loved to do. This turned out to be exactly what the audience was looking for.

I created a four-hour workshop on this theme. I knew I had good material, but I was still nervous about my ability to deliver a solid presentation to a room of three hundred skeptics. Then I had a second epiphany. Salespeople hated marketing presentations because they never trusted marketing people; I was about to change that and I knew my style would win their trust. By pulling this off, I'd turn a room full of seasoned skeptics into a room full of future job references. I started thinking about the presentation as one big job interview. Since Computervision was failing, most of the people in the audience would be working somewhere else within a year, and wherever they ended up, there might be an opportunity for me as a marketing executive.

This change of mindset, combined with good content, made the meeting a rousing success. Of course, Computervision continued to fail and I left a year later to pursue a better job for more money. The people in the audience that day ended up helping me win my next position, as well as the one after that. It did turn out to be a big job interview.

While an important presentation is like a job interview, there is one exception: the audience seldom gets to ask you tough questions you can't answer. You control the agenda; you make your case, back it up, and declare your conclusions. Ideally, you'll be able to get off the stage while everyone is still clapping. People who witness a great presentation become job leads for the rest of your career.

Special Skills Earn Extra Privileges

The best thing about establishing yourself as a good speaker is the freedom that goes with it. Since your boss and coworkers probably fear public speaking, they see your skills as a special gift they can't understand; it becomes a sort of super natural power. But as long as you're saving them from having to do it themselves, they'll give you broad latitude to modify your work habits before and after a big presentation. Paul, who I mentioned earlier, was the first person I knew to really exploit this. He lived on the south side of Boston and had a dreadful commute. He was always looking for an excuse to work at home, and eventually discovered "presentation prep" as an excellent standing excuse. Once or twice a month, he'd call

113

to tell me that he had a major presentation coming up and that there were too many distractions in the office for him to prep there. He would ask if it would be okay to work at home, where he could concentrate better. Although I was skeptical of this ploy, I always allowed it because I knew that I would likely get a letter or a phone call in the next few days commending Paul's performance. Occasionally, presentations would be so "draining" that Paul would need a half a day off to recuperate. As long as his presentations kept earning rave reviews, I gave him all the room he needed to make them happen; it was helping my career as well.

Becoming A Presentation Master

By now I hope I've sold you on the career benefits of developing a proficiency in public speaking. Of course, I haven't done a thing to help you to improve your presentation skills or quell your stage fright. But hopefully I've gotten you motivated to stop running away from speaking engagements and start figuring out how to build the skills you need to become a master.

Most of the good speakers I've known weren't born that way; they simply learned how to do it, one step at a time. They will tell you that the fear never goes away, but you can learn how to channel the nervous energy to improve your performance on the podium. With a little faith, a few techniques, and live practice in safe situations, you can become a very good presenter. Fortunately for you, the difference between a good presenter and a master is not as big as you may think.

Tackle The Fear First

If you're afraid to speak, you won't be much of a speaker, so let's focus on calming your nerves at the podium before anything else. First, let's look at the root cause of fear of public speaking. In general, stage fright is just another version of fear of the unknown.

Specifically, you get scared because you don't know:

1. If the audience is actually interested in what you're talking about.

2. If they know more about the topic than you do and will thus be disinterested and think you're a fool for telling them something they already know.

3. If you are speaking over their heads. You fear you will lose them in the first five minutes because they can't follow you, and then watch them doze off or leave the room in the middle of your presentation.

4. If you'll just freeze up and stumble or bumble the words coming out of your mouth.

One thing is certain: if you're uncomfortable with the first three anxieties on this list, you're very likely to experience the fourth. The best way to calm these fears is to always start your presentation prep by figuring out who your audience is and what you have to say that they'll find interesting. It sounds so simple, but once you've crossed that bridge, the bulk of your fear will dissipate.

Turn Your Presentation Into A Conversation

If you were able to land a job as a white-collar worker, you can probably hold up your end of a business conversation without breaking into a cold sweat. Conversations are simple; you make a statement, the person you're talking to says something and you respond. You don't have to struggle to come up with words to say, you just open your mouth and they come out.

A big secret to overcoming the fear of public speaking is to trick your brain into thinking that you're having an imaginary conversation and get the words to flow just like they do when you're talking to a friend. To do this, you need to do two things. First, you need to actually get to know two or three people who will be in the audience you're speaking to. This will enable you to actually look at them during your speech and pretend you're having a conversation with just them. Second, you need to design your presentation in such a way as to ask the kinds of questions they have on their minds and then provide the answers through your discourse.

Since your speaking career will probably begin with small audiences, it should be quite easy to contact a few members of the audience ahead of time and talk to them about the topic of your presentation. Figure out how much they know about the subject and what they want to learn from you. Most importantly, get to know them as people, not just strange faces in an audience.

When you get to the room that you'll be speaking in, seek out these people and chat with them ahead of time; it will calm you down. Watch where they sit, and then look at them while you're giving your presentation; it will quell your fear.

Write your speech or presentation according to the flow your imaginary conversation with these people might take. Make a point, raise the questions or issues that your select audience members mentioned, then answer these rhetorical queries through your presentation materials. Before you know it, your words will start to flow as if you were talking to these people in a conversation. In the beginning, you should try to forget the rest of the people in the room and talk directly to those people you know. Most importantly, look at them when you answer a question or issue they raised and you'll see a friendly, nodding face who wants to hear what you have to say and who hopes your speech is a success. With this kind of support in the audience, it will be successful.

If you find it impossible to actually meet with audience members ahead of time, you can come close to achieving the same result through a different means. Spend a lot of time talking to the person who invited you to speak; ask them the same questions and then use the answers they provide to create your imaginary conversation.

The key to conquering your fear of speaking is to systematically eliminate the unknowns that shout in your head while you're trying to make the right words come out of your mouth. Replace the idea that you're speaking to a room full of unknown strangers with the image of a few familiar faces. Soon, those shouts of fear will start to become whispers. You'll still have some anxiety about your speaking, but with this technique you will no longer be scared to death.

Telling Stories Makes You Interesting

Most white-collar presentations are either informative or persuasive. An informative speech involves explaining to people how to do something or reporting the status of your work to your boss, coworkers, or subordinates. In a persuasive presentation you're generally selling a product or an idea to somebody in authority, making a case and hoping they will follow your advice or accept your reasoning.

Once source of fear is that neither of these formats is inherently interesting and your audience may tune out early. That fear alone may generate high levels of anxiety. On the other hand, I find that if I truly believe that the audience will find my speech interesting, I relax. The easiest way to accomplish this is to become a storyteller. People relate to stories. They cover a defined period of time, flow in chronological order, and allow the listeners to easily keep pace. Everyone can sense when you're getting to the end of your story and most people love a happy ending, so make sure you give them one.

Telling stories is generally easier and more fun than giving a status update, teaching people to fill out a form, or pitching your product's bells and whistles. You don't have to be a great presenter if you tell a good story. Remember the Jacques Cousteau show? You could barely understand what he was saying through his broken English, but the stories about undersea exploration were fascinating and his audience loved them.

In 1995, I was Chief Marketing Officer at Concentra, a sales
force automation company in Burlington, Massachusetts. I
had reluctantly agreed to fly to Tokyo, attend a three-day
user group, and give the keynote speech on behalf of the
corporate headquarters. Since the audience was all
Japanese and 8,000 miles away, it was tough to single out
a few people ahead of time and talk to them about a topic.
Instead, I spoke to our local Regional Manager about his
expectations for my presentation and learned that our
customers were very unhappy. They had all bought older
products from the company before we changed strategies
and were suffering from weak customer service. The
Regional Manager wanted me to present our plans to
address their issues and persuade them to buy more
products.

Unfortunately, Concentra had very limited resources and I
didn't have a plan to address their issues. I had to give an
interesting presentation that would make them feel good
about our company and get them motivated to buy more
products in the future. So I told them a story.

I gave them a brief company history refresher and told
them what we'd been doing to raise money and what we
were doing with it. I showed them a picture of our new
building, hard-working engineers, customers attending
training classes, and our new products. My story conveyed
the image of a company that was taking action to make
itself better. Since it was a tale of sorts, it was easy to tell
and easy to follow, even through a translator. The
Japanese were quite happy with my presentation and
decided that they needed to learn more about our new
products. It was more than we had hoped for.

After that I started using storytelling as a framework for
all of my presentations. Instead of presenting new product
features and functions, I'd tell prospective customers an
historical tale about the process we went through to
discover and prioritize the features they wanted and what
we did to make sure they worked well. Or rather than

118

simply give my boss a list of accomplishments and issues every month, I'd tell him about the events that had changed our priorities and why. It was easier to say, more interesting to listen to, and it generally led to a constructive discussion. I learned that telling stories made me comfortable because they always kept the audience interested in what I was saying.

Become The Audience's Ambassador To A Strange Land

Telling stories alone isn't enough to defeat your stage fright; you also have to make these tales interesting. I have found that the best way to craft an interesting story is to position yourself as an ambassador returning from some foreign land with a report about what you found there. In most cases, you'll be telling people something they don't already know, and as long as it relates to the world they live in, they'll generally be quite interested.

In the Computervision sales meeting I mentioned earlier, I was reporting my findings from a place the sales force agreed was quite strange—the corporate headquarters. My real stories about product strengths and weaknesses provided them with a translation from corporate doubletalk into something they could understand. Before the speech, they were frustrated by the maze of Corporate Product Marketing, but with my help, they were able to sift through it and envision winning sales campaigns. Not only did they enjoy my presentation, but from that day forward they also saw me as someone they could call whenever they needed help figuring out something in the strange land of corporate.

In 2001, I took over a product development team for the first time in my career. It was a large organization with over 900 people. The first time I spoke to a room full of engineers they just stared at me like I was from another planet. I never wanted to have this happen again, so I came up with an idea to become their ambassador to the outside world. I'd tell them stories about how their products were being marketed, sold, and ultimately used by customers. They loved to hear this.

After the second presentation, one of my Vice Presidents, Vinay Ambaker, came into my office to thank me for giving his people a great presentation. I asked him why he thought it was so good and he said, "Because you were the first executive who talked to engineers like they were adults, not children."

I actually hadn't changed the way I talked to them at all. I had just told them a story about something they were curious about. Instead of talking about the company's results and markets, I spoke about how the things they had been working on and how they were actually being received in the outside world. These engineers spent their lives creating products and no one had ever come back to talk to them about the fruits of their labor. Doing so was interesting to them and they thought that it was respectful. All I did was figure out what they were curious about and then became their visiting ambassador with a field report.

The best way to conquer your fear of presenting is to come up with a story that you know the audience will enjoy hearing. Audiences always enjoy a story that translates well or explains a mystery for them and you'll enjoy telling them the story.

Profile Dave Lemont
Presentation Mastery Made Simple

> Dave Lemont grew up in Brooklyn, New York. The streets were tough and he learned how to talk his way out of trouble at an early age. He began his career in sales and progressed through marketing into general management. After a number of successful start-ups, Dave started his own consulting business focusing on the execution of key success factors for start-up companies. Much of Dave's success traces back to his unusual, but highly effective, style of presentation.

I met Dave in 1992. He had just joined Computer-vision as a marketing vice president and I was a sales manager in Santa Clara, California. Dave impressed me immediately by the way his straight talk put people at ease. Even more remarkable was the fact that he had the same effect talking to you one-on-one or when addressing an audience of hundreds of people. Dave clearly knew how to make himself comfortable in front of a crowd and how to draw the interest of his audience.

I recently sat down with him and asked him about his unique presentation technique. In particular, I was looking for tricks or techniques that others might adapt to their own style and thereby accelerate their personal presentation mastery. Here are a number of tips from Dave Lemont's presentation play book:

Make Them Laugh Early
"When I hear the audience laugh at something I said, it gives me immediate confidence that my pre-sentation will be a success. Starting a presentation with a joke is as old as water; that's not what I'm talking about. I want to hear them laugh at something original. It has to be current and topical. I usually force myself to wait until 15 or 20 minutes before I start to come up with something funny to say. Ideally, it's about the topic at hand, an audience member, or some high-ranking official in the company. Worst case, I'll pull something out of today's newspaper. The point is, I know people want to let out a good laugh and I know once I hear that, I'm off to giving a great presentation."

Engage the Audience by Name
"I think of a presentation like a prize fight. I need to be loose in order to be on my game. I like to work the crowd right before the presentation starts. I walk around, talk to people, and figure out what's on their mind and what they hope to hear from me. Then once I start talking, I try to weave stories that mention members of the audience into my material. Not only does this command the attention of the people I mention, I also think it invokes a subliminal

response from everyone else. Once people hear me mention the name of someone they know, they listen more intently, just in case I call out their name next."

Use Body Language
"I'm left handed and I know that I'll be more relaxed on the left side of the stage, so I always try and set up that way. I use a variety of different postures throughout the speech, to build the audience's curiosity and let them know I'm in charge. I like to start my presentations sitting on a stool or speaking from the podium and then walk out to the middle of the stage as my confidence builds. Walking into the audience with a wireless mike is even better."

Always Script the Close
"Even though I still get a little scared giving a big speech, I know that I can look forward to a tremendous physical rush when it's over! In fact, my anticipation of that rush drives me to be a better speaker. The best way to assure that I will have an exciting finish is to carefully plan my closing remarks. I try to end on an emotional note, with a forward-looking or uplifting message, and try to inspire my audience to do something meaningful. I write down the words I hope to say, practice them, and commit them to memory. Knowing that I have prepared a killer close keeps me going in the middle of my speech and builds excitement for the rush that comes at the end."

Be Yourself
"The biggest mistake I see lousy presenters make is trying to be someone they're not. If you're an expert, be THE EXPERT, but if you're not, just be a curious observer and talk about what you've learned. Don't try and fool people—it never works. I know that I give the best presentations when my confidence is highest, and in order to feel confident, I have to always be myself and speak from my heart."

Developing Your Game

Strategy Six does not purport to teach you everything you need to know about how to master the art of presentation;

it's just one chapter in Career Secret Sauce. To truly develop your skills, I'd recommend you join Toastmasters International, where you can hone your ability in front of people you will probably never meet again. There are also a number of books that cover this topic exclusively. One of my favorites is Malcom Kusner's "Presentations for Dummies." Unlike most of the "Dummies" books that just introduce the basics of a subject, Kusner hits on almost all of the major principles. Of course, I have a few tricks of my own that I'd like to share and you probably won't find these anywhere else.

Six Rules For Presentation Excellence

There are a few secret rules about making your presentation great that are seldom taught in workshops or found in books. I've learned about them through my own experiences as my presentation skills have evolved. Apply these rules to your presentations and regardless of the quality of your content or strength of delivery, people will think you're a better presenter. Most of these rules apply to both speeches and presentations made with PowerPoint slides. I've found that virtually all successful business speaking is accompanied by a slide show of some sort.

Rule #1—Always Write A Script

Nobody wants to hear someone read a speech; it's annoying and generally dull. For this reason most people skip the most important rule of good speaking and fail to script the words they plan to say ahead of time. I have always scripted new material before I use it, but I never read it when I'm speaking. And without fail, 90 percent of the words I planned to speak end up coming out of my mouth when the show starts.

When I script my presentation, I make a conscious effort to think through the points I need to make, when I need to make them, and how I'd like to verbalize them. It might take me an hour or two to script a 30-minute presentation, but that process somehow records the words I'm hoping to say into my subconscious mind. When the lights come on and I need to start talking, my mind—plays back the recording I scripted earlier and I can almost see the words in my head. I have skipped scripting a few times and found myself stumbling for words, even after years as a master presenter.

Don't just take my word for it; do it! First practice giving the speech with the written script in front of you, and then try without it. Practicing is just another insurance policy for good speaking. The more you practice the script you wrote, the deeper the words get burned into your subconscious. Practice will also allow you to gauge how long it will take you to deliver your speech—a critical rule we'll talk about later. I always rehearse a major presentation and often practice new material.

Rule #2—Memorize Strategically

Some people will attempt to memorize their entire speech. If you have such a memory, go for it, but most people don't. Whenever I have attempted to memorize every word, I end up putting pressure on myself and increasing my level of anxiety. However, a little memorization can be a very good thing.

For starters, you should always memorize the first three or four sentences of your speech. That way, you know you'll get off to a good start and you can relax during the first 30 seconds, look around the room, and start thinking about what comes next.

If you noticed while scripting that there were points or slides that seemed difficult to explain, you may want to memorize a few of those lines to make sure you hit them cleanly when you get to that point.

Finally, if memorizing is one of your skills, you can also learn the first sentence and the last sentence you hope to use for every slide.

Rule #3—Break Your Speaking Rhythm

With all this scripting, practice and memorization, it's pretty easy to turn your well-planned speech into a

124

monotonous drone. You want to get all the words out and get off the podium as fast as possible, so you start talking faster than normal and the next thing you know you sound like you're singing a one-note song. That's when your audience nods off for a good nap.

The way to avoid this is simple: just pause for effect every few minutes. Take a breath, look around the room, check your notes, mentally queue up the next three of four lines, and then jump back in where you left off. When a speaker pauses, a little bell goes off in the minds of your audience. People generally anticipate that a pause in a speech precedes an important line, so they stop daydreaming and start paying attention again.

Another trick that has a similar impact is to ask a rhetorical question, pause, and then answer it. This probably works because it subconsciously brings the audience back to grade school, and the fear that the teacher might call on them to answer the rhetorical question. The little spike of adrenaline will almost always wake them up.

This applies to the pace of your slide transitions as well. If you establish a pattern of advancing a new bullet every ninety seconds and a new slide every four minutes, your audience will drift away to the rhythm. They can read your bullet faster than you can speak about it, and once they've gotten your point, they'll start daydreaming until the next ninety seconds is up and a new bullet appears. To avoid this, have some slides that are only up for ten seconds and let others linger for five minutes. Fly through some bullets as fast as you can get the words out, and have other slides with no bullets at all. Mix it up and you'll keep your audience on their toes trying to figure out what you're going to say or do next. They'll think you're an interesting speaker.

Rule #4—Never Run Over

When asked to give a presentation always find out how long they would like you to speak and whether or not you should take questions. Assume five minutes of Q&A for every 20 minutes of presentation. If you have a thirty-minute slot, give a twenty-minute presentation and then ask for questions. If there are no questions and people get a little break, they'll appreciate you for giving it to them.

Your job as a speaker is to convey your message in a coherent fashion and in the prescribed time slot and then to get off the stage. Finishing your presentation five minutes early is infinitely better than finishing five minutes late. When you run over on time, you abuse everyone. Some people may have to leave exactly at the scheduled conclusion of your speech. Run over and you force them to awkwardly get up and leave the room while you're still waxing on. You also cut into the time of anyone who follows you on the agenda. They'll resent it and so will the person responsible for keeping the agenda on schedule. Finally, every second you run over tests your audience's patience. They know that you failed to finish on time, but they don't know if you're almost done, or if you lost your watch and are going to babble on for fifteen more minutes. They may start thinking about what they were planning to do next and whether or not they should stand up and walk out while you're still talking. They will stop paying attention to what you're saying and listen for cues that you're almost done.

Running over is always a bad idea and beyond that, it is the mark of a poor presenter.

Rule #5—Signal Your Finish—Draw Applause

No matter how good your presentation was, everyone who heard it will think it was much better if people clap at the end. If you end your presentation with a quick "thank you, are there any questions?" you'll never enjoy the satisfaction of a hearty round of applause. That ending always results in dead silence as people consider whether or not to ask a question and look around nervously to see if anyone else is going to be so bold. In order to draw applause, you have to signal your finish, pause, and wait for the applause. And only after the applause ceases should you ask for questions. Here's an example of a solid ending:

"In conclusion, I'd like to thank you all for giving me this opportunity to share my story with you. You've been a very gracious audience and if you're ever in my neck of the woods, stop by. I'd love to show you what we do first hand…"

If anyone out there was even thinking about clapping, you just gave him a ten second wake-up call. Everyone in the room is poised and all it will take is one happy camper to get it all started. It can even be initiated by one of your subordinates in the room planted for just such an assignment. Once the thunder stops, you can sheepishly look at your watch, thank them once again, and ask for questions. Of course, in those rare occasions where this trick doesn't work, you simply cut straight to the Q&A.

Rule #6—Follow the Speaking Food Chain

By now you should be motivated and reasonably educated on how to become a great presenter. You may even have a topic or a speaking opportunity you're ready to take on. The fastest way to crash and burn as a presenter is to take on an important assignment before you're ready. Speaking to a room of twenty new employees about what your department does is quite different from talking to Wall Street analysts about the competitive strengths of your company's new product. The first group will eat up everything you say and the second group will eat you alive.

If you're just now committing to developing your presentation skills, start off small and move up the food chain as fast as you comfortably can. Toastmasters is a great venue for failsafe practice, as are internal training sessions and orientations. Always be sure you know what you're doing before you speak to customers, the media, or industry analysts.

You'll also find it more challenging to speak from a stage than from the end of a table. A podium with a microphone can be scary, and a wireless mike on an open stage is even worse. The biggest hurdle you'll have to face as a public speaker will come when the audience gets so big that they need bright house lights just so they can see you. When this happens, you won't be able to see anyone beyond the first row, just a bank of bright lights glaring on your forehead. Always ask how big the audience is before you agree to give a presentation. If it's over two hundred and fifty people, be prepared for full sensory deprivation on stage.

This One Is There For The Taking

Every one of the Nine Strategies in *Career Secret Sauce* is special, but nothing can help your career more than mastering the art of presentation. It will dramatically enhance your job security, increase your eligibility for promotion, and help you build a reputation that will influence headhunters to continuously recruit you for better jobs. It's not easy in the beginning, but contrary to most challenges, it gets easier over time. And unlike a lot of the brass rings you'll chase in your quest for a great career, there will be few people elbowing you to grab this one.

PHASE
THREE

Effectively Navigate Raises, Promotions, and Job Changes

STRATEGY SEVEN

Promotionology; The Art Of The Raise

We've heard all the lines: "It's only money," "Money can't buy happiness," and "Money is the Root of All Evil." Truer words were never spoken. You get your first taste of this intoxicating substance before you hit high school: cutting lawns, babysitting, or delivering newspapers for extra cash. If you're lucky, you might have even gotten an allowance and learned firsthand how quick money can disappear. It's easy in the beginning: all of your money goes for candy and movies. Your food, shelter, and just about everything else comes at "no charge" from Mommy and Daddy. Then you get a driver's license and want to buy a car; or you get to college and have to pay tuition or take on a college loan. Now it's getting serious. Finally you graduate and get a real job. When you see your first paycheck you think you're rolling in dough. Then you move away from home, rent an apartment, and starting paying bills. Suddenly the old adage "struggling to make ends meet" starts to have real meaning. Just wait until you get married and have kids. At that point money will become the bane of your very existence.

While we generally work for reasons that go beyond money, barely a day goes by without thinking that you're underpaid. The downside of an inadequate paycheck is that you can't pay your bills or at a minimum buy what

131

you want. You look around at others who seem to be more comfortable and feel inferior or cheated.

A new raise is euphoric, but it's a temporary euphoria; within weeks you start thinking about your next raise or bonus. The upside is that when you do get a good raise or bonus it's one of the few times in your career that you'll ever experience unqualified personal satisfaction about your performance.

Strategy Seven, Promotionology; The Art of The Raise, may be the most important chapter in Career Secret Sauce. You must understand this game in order to play it well. If you choose not to play, coworkers who learn how to manipulate the system for their own advantage will likely pass you by. Most importantly, your self-esteem and ultimate happiness is at risk if you fail to comprehend this complex topic and take it all too personally. It's only money.

Salary Administration 101

I never worked in the Human Resources department and I can't say I regret it. From a distance, it looks like a lot of fluff work and handholding, but HR professionals do have two important functions in any organization. The first is to make sure managers play fair when they fire or lay-off an employee; and the second is to administer the salary plan for the company. They are the police that manage Salary Administration.

It may appear to the naked eye that starting salaries and raises are all chosen at random (and in very small companies this may be often true). But as soon as a company hires someone to "do personnel," offer letters, pay scales, and annual increases take on the air of a scientific endeavor. Large companies and government organizations can make this topic extremely complicated, but this is just a basic primer, so we'll skip the details associated with large-scale enterprises.

Before we can start discussing how to "work the system" to your advantage, allow me to cover the basics of Salary Administration 101.

Job Grades

The first foundation of every salary administration plan is the job grade. Job grades are created by taking every single employee in the company and classifying them into 10 to 15 groups. The concept is that each group of job classes has a similar compensation level both within the company and across the industry. Each job grade is assigned a broad salary range that theoretically represents the minimum and maximum that everyone who holds a job in that group is paid. Under healthy economic conditions, salary ranges are increased once a year. In theory, everyone in a given job grade is entitled to the same salary. Job grades are designed to normalize pay across similar jobs within a department and dissimilar jobs across the company or industry. The Director of Accounting may be considered a pay grade 10 and so may a Senior Product Manager in marketing. Since these two jobs have the same pay grade, they each have the same salary range.

The Salary Budget

We all believe that we should be paid fairly for the job we do, regardless of the financial condition of our employer or the economy at large. Unfortunately, that is not the case. Most companies strive to pay people what they deserve, but in reality, it's a secondary concern. The first priority is to live within the annual budget for salaries and salary increases, even if it means underpaying employees. Managing this budget and the underlying process is where the HR department earns its keep!

At the beginning of every year, companies set a budget for all of the expenditures they plan to make. In most cases, the top-down budget for payroll and salaries is the biggest single line item in this budget. This budget represents the total dollar amount planned for all raises for every employee. Salary is considered the most controllable of all

133

expenses and companies will do everything in their power to avoid overspending. There are two knobs that management can turn to control this enormous outlay. They can limit (or even reduce) the number of employees on the payroll, or they can limit the amount of money set aside for salary increases (also known as the Raise Budget).

In setting the Raise Budget, companies look at inflation, projected profits for the coming year, and occasionally employee morale. They then take the actual salary expenditure "run rate" at the end of the previous year, bump it up for planned new hires, and figure out how much they can afford to spend in the coming year. The dollar budget is usually communicated in the form of a percentage. This percentage should be close to the overall salary inflation rate in the company's industry and represent the average raise available for all employees.

Allocating The Budget For Raises

The top-down budget then gets divvyed up by department. This creates a "raise pool" for the manager to allocate across all employees. Sometimes every department gets the same percentage budget, but often they differ. If your department is small, your boss doesn't have a lot in the pool to fiddle around with. If you are in a large department with a lot of overpaid coworkers, your boss may be fat with cash. If your group loses a lot of people right after the annual salary budget get sets, there may be even more cash to dole out in raises for those who stick around and get the work done.

Of course, these salary and compensations budgets are never absolute. Just because your boss has a fat salary increase budget on paper, doesn't mean that her boss won't come and grab it to give to another department. But, if you're personally carrying the weight of coworkers who've resigned or overpaid prima donnas who won't do the dirty work, odds are pretty good that your boss has a stash of money he can use to give you an extraordinary raise.

Pay For Performance

The final leg in the salary administration game is a tool used to rank one employee against another. This is to make sure managers pay for performance and don't simply give everyone the average percentage in order to avoid a confrontation with underperformers. The simplest tool is just a form to "rank and stack" employees. Managers are forced to rank employees such that their best employee is number one on the list and so on down the line. Other companies use a Salary Increase Matrix, or a Pay Grid. The Matrix or Grid typically has 4 quadrants that correspond to the recommended annual salary increase for different employee situations. The rationale behind the Pay Grid is to force managers to pigeonhole employees into one of four categories inside the matrix. Each has a salary increase percentage associated with it and that is the official raise guideline.

Here is a typical Pay Grid with sample raise guidelines and my personal commentary about the characteristics associated with being in that box.

Highest Paid

Raise Range 0%	Raise Range 3 - 5%	
You're overpaid and you're not doing squat!	*You're doing a good job and we're paying you well...*	**Top Performers**
Raise Range 1 - 3%	Raise Range 5 - 10%	
You're not doing much and you're getting paid what you deserve...	*You're doing a great job, we're paying you peanuts, and we both know it!*	

This matrix is pretty simple, but they can get more complicated. I once worked at a company that ranked employees on a scale of 1 to 5 along two dimensions: competency and commitment. The goal was to force managers to identify their most skilled workers and then go on record effectively guaranteeing their loyalty to the organization. The top employees were called "double nickels" because they were ranked 5 along both dimensions. This system got perverted once the company hit hard times. They froze salaries, started laying people off, and anyone who was not a double nickel was considered expendable; managers had to jump through hoops defending anyone who they scored as less than a "5" for commitment.

While it's useful to know what the pay for performance methodology is that your company uses, it's more important to simply know that one exists. Recognizing that your boss will have take money from someone else to sweeten your salary can help you to rationalize something that's less than you think you deserve. This will help you to avoid beating yourself up for a raise that is less than you hoped to receive. Furthermore, you really need to know your pay grade and salary range before you can assess if your raise is good or bad. The absolute size of your raise is not as important as what it really tells you about the current state of your career, your prospects for promotion, or threats to your job security.

If you are at the bottom of the salary range and receive a big raise, don't get too excited. You may think that you're doing really well, but it's just the system compensating you for taking such a low starting salary. Do not misinterpret it as a strong vote of confidence from a grateful boss. Ignore the size of the raise and focus on the words you hear when your boss talks about your performance. On the other hand, if you are at the top of your pay grade, your prospects for a raise are pretty bleak—no matter how great a job your boss thinks you're doing. In this case, don't get discouraged by a puny raise. Probe for feedback on your performance and start working on getting promoted. You may be great at what you do, but you cannot loiter around the top of the salary range without putting your career at risk. Suppose your boss quits, gets fired, or promoted out of your chain of command. Now you have a new boss who's going to take one look at your big salary and assume that you're nothing but "fat" waiting to be trimmed. Suppose your new boss turns out to be a former peer, who has moved up quickly and may be making less than you! Now you're in real danger.

The point is, where you are in the salary range for your job is the most vital piece of information you can get to tell you how secure you are in your current position.

Busting The Pay Plan

Although you should be concerned about your job security if you're sitting at the top of the salary range for your job, the problem may take care of itself without having to lift a finger. Pay plans get busted and reset on a regular basis. The catalyst for busting can vary. Sometimes, it happens because a big guy upstairs really wants to hire someone who costs a lot more than everyone else in the pay grade, so everyone in the job grade gets bumped up to a new salary range. Or a department might be faced with rampant turnover and management needs to jump through hoops to keep the rest of the team in place, so he reclassifies the top performers to a higher pay grade. Or your old boss just got fired and the new boss needs to employ desperate measures to keep everyone from walking out the door. If you find yourself in any of these situations, your antennae should go up and you should be on the lookout for a change in job grade and new salary range.

The second easiest way to get bumped is to win an "in job" promotion. Here your boss effectively adds the word "senior" to your job title and gives you a raise. Your job responsibilities don't change; you just get more money and a more impressive title. By moving people up through in-job promotions every few years, your boss gets to keep

137

good people under his control without having to risk giving them any real increase in responsibilities. He can also avoid having to promote one peer to management and risk alienating the rest of the team. Of course most everyone knows it's not a real promotion, but you will get a bigger raise and decent fodder for your résumé.

Another way to bust the pay plan is called an "early review." If you can convince your boss that you're a high performer and under paid (the lower right hand quadrant), and/or a threat to walk out the door for greener pastures, you can often negotiate a second salary review (raise) in the same year. If you've been applying "The List" time management technique, we covered in Strategy Five, your boss knows that you're good and vital to the performance of the team. He also knows that you could step in and replace one of his overpaid seat warmers in a heartbeat and probably get more work done in less time. All you have to do is get yourself in a situation where you and he are talking about how to "address your salary inequity." Then, you can suggest a series of early reviews to close the gap.

My First Promotion

In 1976, I was approached about my first promotion. It was from Production Control Clerk to Inventory Control Coordinator, working for a guy named Marcellus Stamps— Mars for short. It also included supervising a subordinate. I was flattered to be considered for promotion. I had accepted the paltry starting salary of $125 a week in order to get my foot in the door and had a minor chip on my shoulder. A promotion would give me a chance to earn the salary I deserved, so the first question I asked Mars was: "What does this job pay?"

I don't think Mars had done his homework and he didn't know that I was working for substandard pay and quickly replied, "$175 a week."

This translated into $50 more a week or a 40 percent raise. I saw my inadequate salary situation being corrected in one fell swoop, and immediately asked, "When can I start?"

I enjoyed the job and Mars turned out to be a great guy, except for one thing. Every Friday I'd open my paycheck looking for my raise, just to be disappointed with the same old $125. This went on for months and finally I complained and learned that my paperwork was sitting on Mars' boss's desk. A few weeks later he called me into a closed-door meeting and said, "I have your raise."

Being a youngster with no experience in salary matters, I was completely unprepared for what happened next: "Your salary is being increased to $135/week," he said, "retroactive to the day you started the new job for **merit**, and increased to $155/week effective today for the **promotion**."

"What happened to the $175/week I was promised months ago?" I screamed in my head. "How can this be happening? I've been doing the job for months! Why is the promotion effective today?"

Emotionally floored, I started babbling about going to personnel and filing a complaint or some other immature nonsense when my good buddy Mars said, "Do that and I'll fire you myself." I quickly sobered up, apologized for acting up and thanked him for the raise.

On that day I learned firsthand the importance of getting the highest starting salary possible. Even if your boss agrees that you're underpaid, no one in the company is going to allow him to give you a 40 percent increase. Since all of your future increases will be limited to a percentage of your starting pay, you want to get as close to a fair starting salary as possible. Most bosses are pressured to pay you as little as they can get away with, but you just have stick to your guns; if you cave in the beginning, you'll pay for it for years to come.

The Starting Salary Game

From that day in 1976 forward, I became relentless in negotiating as much money as possible on every new job I accepted. Once you've had your first job in your chosen field, it's a lot easier to negotiate a new salary. After all, changing jobs is both stressful and risky. No one expects you to switch without getting more money. How much more is part of the negotiation, but 10-15 percent is a good rule of thumb. This also means that you have to tell your future employer what you're currently making before you can start negotiating.

After working for twenty years, I negotiated a new job with Aspect Development paying $160,000/year. I had negotiated with the President, Joe Prang, and argued based on my current pay (in Massachusetts) and the higher cost of living in Northern California. Joe used a sketchy local salary survey to make the case that his offer was fair. After I accepted, their recruiter Paul Deppmeier said to me, "We are very pleased that you've accepted our offer. Welcome aboard! By the way, we have a policy of getting a copy of every new hires prior year W2 statement for your file. It's just a formality."

Paul was the first one to ever pull this trick question on me and fortunately it was probably the first time in my life that I hadn't embellished my salary from my old job—just a little. Exaggerating what you make to bait a better offer is just human nature; after all, we want to get paid as much as possible. Even if the new guy was willing to pay you $20 an hour, he'll probably only offer you $18, if you tell him that you're making $15 an hour in your old job. Of course if you stretched the truth a little and told him you were making $17.50 and then he asks for your W2, you're in deep trouble. The best thing that might happen is that he cuts your offer. More likely, he'll tear up your offer letter and tell you they don't hire liars. If you've already resigned from your last job you're in deep, deep trouble. When you go in for your initial interview for a potential new job, the very last question you're planning to ask is,

"What does this job pay?" Even if you're curious, you know it's an inappropriate question to ask until you understand the job and they've shown strong interest in making an offer. You won't hear a word about starting salary from your potential employer until they're ready to put an offer in writing, but that doesn't mean they won't ask you about your current salary a whole lot sooner—often early in the initial interview. In fact if you're going through an outside recruiter, don't be surprised if he asks you over the phone before even scheduling a meeting.

If you haven't prepared for this question, you will be faced with an instant dilemma. Do you tell the truth, refuse to answer, or make up a number?

First off, you should never lie, particularly about a verifiable fact. What was on your W2 for the prior year is a fact. If they ask you to prove it, you have nowhere to hide. You can round up to the nearest ten thousand, but that's about it. If you choose to answer the question that's you're only viable option. On the other hand, there are a number of ways to respond that are truthful and yet enable you to dance around the question and retain your ability to negotiate a good deal when the time comes:

1. Defer the Question—"Whoa, we just started talking. I can understand why you'd like to know that, but I'm old fashioned about private matters like salary. Let's talk about the job and my potential fit before we get involved in salary negotiations." This is a reasonable stall tactic. You'll get points for being smooth, but you'll still have to answer the question later and you may have sent up a red flag that you're hiding something. It's best to use this tactic as a desperate measure.

2. Leverage the Question—"Last year's earnings were disappointing, that's one of the reasons I'm looking for a new job." The problem with this response is that it will make you sound like a mercenary. Of course, if

that's true, or you're looking for a job in sales, it's not a bad way to handle the question.

3. Change the Question—"Last year I made $ ____, but that was a long time ago. I performed above expectations and they took care of me. Let me tell you what I'll make this year." You can then go on to predict your salary for the coming year. You can predict a fat raise, you can predict an early review, and you can predict a large bonus. You're not lying; you're not even embellishing. You're simply making a rosy forecast about your prospects for the future. You know it's rosy and they know it's rosy. That's the beauty of this strategy. You tell the truth (always a good thing), but you convince them that it will take a higher number to get you to move. If you play it right, you also demonstrate confidence and the ability to "think on your feet."

Promotionology

Negotiating a fat starting salary and busting the pay plan is all well and good. These are great little tactics, but if this were a baseball game, they'd be the equivalent of stealing a base. It may help you score a run now and then, but it won't win the game. Home runs win ball games. When it comes to your career, promotions are home runs. They are the best and the fastest ways to grow your salary, establish job security, and give you more control over your time.

The first thing you have to understand about Promotionology is that big promotions seldom go to the brightest and hardest working candidate. Executives see teams as living, breathing organisms. Organizations consume resources, produce outputs, and evolve over time. When they select a new manager for a team, they consider how that promotion will affect the rest of the team. If the team is a little lazy or dull, they may promote a very bright, hard working candidate to shake them up, but this is more the exception than the rule. In most cases, managers are more concerned about the downside risks of promoting someone that the team rejects than they are with the fleeting hope that they can turn a team of laggards into dynamos by forcing them to work for a Type A personality. Sadly, most promotions are designed to maintain the status quo (while hoping to get a little upside in the process).

The First Rule Of Promotionology—Always Be The Least Hated

Most promotions go to the person who the team hates the least as their potential new boss. Why do I say hated the least versus liked the most? Very few people like the idea of a new boss, unless it's going to be them! Most people get really emotional when a former peer becomes the new boss. And that's usually what happens when companies promote from within. The classic reaction to discovering that a former peer is your new boss is to update your résumé and look for a new job. However, some peer promotions are less traumatic than others. The best way to get promoted is to establish yourself as the least controversial candidate. Simply put, your goal is to be the last one standing when your peers mentally eliminate all of the other people on the team they would hate to work for.

There are a number of ways to become the least hated future boss. Chances are you'll be competing with ambitious people for every promotion. Most ambitious people are obsessed with themselves, the things they're working on or what they have accomplished. They think it's a waste of time to study the work of coworkers, let alone compliment their efforts. Don't be like them. Develop a habit of publicly recognizing everyone around you for the good work they do. You'll instantly separate yourself from the pack of self-obsessed ambitious coworkers and make a lot of friends. This doesn't mean be a kiss-up. It just means pay attention to what others are doing and don't be afraid to acknowledge someone else's good work. If someone comes up with a clever way of doing something, ask them about it. In staff meetings, remind other team members about the good work of others. Most importantly, spread it around. If you simply hurdle praise on the top performers, you're just fueling their egos. They don't need your praise and you may be inadvertently signalling your boss that you'd be willing to report to them. But if you go the extra mile to recognize the lesser-appreciated members of the team, you'll win more hearts and minds than you can imagine. They will trust you more than those around you and your boss will appreciate your contribution to the overall morale of the team.

The Second Rule Of Promotionology—Save Someone

Back in 1983, I spent a little time on the strategy team at Prime Computer. The job really wasn't my cup of tea. There was virtually no action, just a lot of research and pontification. The big event was the fall board meeting, where each strategist stood up and preached to the Board of Directors about some burning issue facing the company, rattled off a few alternative strategic options and then made a recommendation for dealing with it. This was before the days of PowerPoint and I was about halfway through my overhead slides when I realized that I was missing one of the key ones. I went to the next slide and did my best to avoid the look of panic. There was a woman on the team that I had never been too crazy about—Ellen. But fortunately for me, Ellen picked up on my anxiety, went over to my stuff, found the missing slide, and gracefully handed it to me just in time for me to lay it on the projector without missing a beat. Ellen had saved my presentation and my career. It's been decades and I've never forgotten it. She won a fan for life.

As you cruise through your career, you'll see a lot of people about to get burned in the line of duty. The natural tendency is to stand back and watch the disaster in action. Do not do it! Step in and try and save that person's career life. It's a good thing to do, and they'll never forget you for it. If you can save someone and no one else but them notices, that's even better. If you can save everyone on the team before the next promotion, you may actually find yourself in a position where peers like the idea of you becoming the new boss.

The Third Rule Of Promotionology—Send The Boss Your Plan

Let's assume that you've been generously awarding thoughtful praise to your peers, and you've saved more people than you can count on one hand. Suddenly an opportunity for a promotion presents itself and you decide to throw your hat in the ring. The first thing you do is to formally apply for the job. Usually you start with a visit to HR, followed up by an interview with the hiring manager. As in all interviews, you must sell yourself and gather intelligence about the new job. The most important thing to know is the hiring manager's goals for the new candidate. Some managers will come right out and tell you what they're looking to accomplish, others need to be helped along with probing questions like the ones we discussed in Strategy Three.

Once you've got this information, craft an email to the hiring manager and present your plan for the new job. Your email should refer to his stated objectives. You should include some personal insights about the challenges of getting it done; show off your "street knowledge" of the team and the nuances of the current situation. Also, you should present any relevant experience you have that might better qualify you to make it all happen. It's important to send the plan within 24 hours of the meeting. I like to send it out very late the night of the interview to demonstrate that I'm totally committed and willing to put in long hours to achieve success. If this doesn't win you the job, it will certainly put you at the top of the list for the next promotion.

The Fourth Rule Of Promotionology—Don't Go Changing

That final rule of Promotionology comes into play after you've won the job. One of the biggest mistakes I see people make is to start acting like a different person once they've been promoted. They try to test their new power, treat former peers like inferiors, and start buddying up to their new higher-ranking peers, as if they have equal power and influence in the organization, when they don't. You may not realize it, but you will be under a hidden microscope following every promotion. Former peers are watching and hoping you screw up. As a potential "fast mover", your new contemporaries will be sizing you up as a potential competitor for their next promotion. And of course the guy who promoted you will be watching to make sure he didn't make a mistake. If you start acting like you've finally arrived at a coveted level, you'll probably find that it is the last level you'll ever achieve! Keep in mind that you should already be looking for your next promotion and you need to start acting that way immediately. Start handing out gracious praise and looking for people to save among your new coworkers. Build your new "List" and start working it. Pay special attention to the people you passed on the way up. They may become undercover references for you down the road.

Profile Jay Ennesser
Promotionology at IBM

> In some ways, Jay Ennesser's life has been a throwback to the good old days. He has spent his entire career at the same company, his father worked there, so did his little league coach. Jay even worked there during summer breaks at college. What can Jay's career story of yesteryear possibly teach us about the dynamic job market of the new millennium? For starters, Jay and his dad didn't exactly work in a coal mine, they worked for IBM; one of the world's finest companies and a global leader in technology. More significant, as king of the hill, IBM has been forced to "reinvent itself" multiple times over the last few decades and that made it a very demanding career environment.

> Reinventing the Corporation is one of those nineties terms that sounds nice at first, but then turns out to be quite the opposite. Globalization, emerging technologies, and competitive pressure drive

corporate reinvention and it almost always translates
into cost cutting; letting people go.

For 28 years Jay has worked in this career crucible.
Not only has he survived, he's thrived. Starting out as
computer programmer in 1980, he's steadily climbed
the ladder and today he's a full-fledged vice
president. Not only that, but he's parlayed his career
success to get out of the cold winters of New York
and now calls beautiful Scottsdale, Arizona his home.

I recently joined Jay for a cup of coffee in his desert
home. He shared his secrets for steady career
growth, job security and personal freedom in a tough
corporate environment.

Work on the Production Line for a Day
"One of my first real assignments involved building a
new computer system for analyzing test data and
quality control for semiconductor manufacturing in
Burlington, Vermont. Traditionally, system design
consisted of endless meetings, numerous flow charts
on white boards and hours of pontificating about the
nuances of the process. I didn't have the patience for
that. While these traditional approaches eventually
resulted in a good design, it seemed like it took
forever. I wanted to accelerate the process, so why
not go to the source? I went down to the production
line, put on a dust free "bunny suit" and mask, then
spent a day working with the people producing
semiconductors. I actually lived a day in the world
we were automating. Two great things came out of
this. First, I really learned the process and the true
drivers for a successful system design. Second, I
instantly gained a reputation with management as a
smart, down-to-earth guy, who was willing to roll up
his sleeves. This was a great lesson and one that I
constantly deployed with every new job I took on."

Always Look Beyond the Department Silos
"My second big promotion was in charge of the Tools
and Measurement Systems group. We were in the
process of rewriting everything written for the IBM
Series 1 architecture to operate on the PC. This was
the first job I had managing a group of college

educated professional workers. Although I'd only been at IBM for a few years, I had already noticed artificial boundaries emerging between departments. Everyone thought that their department was the center of the universe. This made cross functional collaboration very difficult. Back then we called these silos. Like a smokestack, everything went up the pipe, never down, and never across to other silos. This just didn't make sense to me and I started looking beyond our little smokestack to see how we effected other departments. One day an opportunity came up for a volunteer job as a JAD Leader. JAD stood for Joint Application Development and it involved assembling cross sections of employees and working out a common design for a new computer system. Again, not only did this process make me a better, more versatile employee, it also put me on the map with senior managers as a guy who could lead a diverse team to a common goal and keep everyone happy."

"This eventually led to a promotion to corporate IBM in Somers New York. This was my first job working with the external world and perhaps the most interesting assignment was being assigned to Sematech, a US consortium of semiconductor companies assembled to combat the growing threat from Japan. Sitting at a table with people from IBM's competitors like Hewlett Packard or AMD was probably the ultimate in terms of breaking down silos."

Be the Quarterback, not the Captain
"I remember one of my bosses in the late eighties saying to me 'Jay, you take care of me.' He didn't mean that I was running for coffee or washing his car. He meant that I provided him with a connection to what was going on in his organization and I was watching his back. I think it goes back to my days playing football. I was never the kind of rah-rah guy who wanted to be captain, but I loved being quarterback. I always took great pride in being able to take the coach's game plan and then explain to the rest of team in a way that they could successfully execute. I think this skill has a lot to do with the job

security I've enjoyed over the years. Managers will do almost anything to protect their "quarterback," and the other players always loved me because I always gave them the winning plays."

Create Visibility for Your Team
"I've talked about getting noticed by management as a key to getting ahead, but it's a little more than that. If all you're doing is getting yourself noticed, you'll end up going up in flames as a self promoter. I think the key is to generate visibility for your team's accomplishments, not your own. Everyone will figure out that you're a key contributor to the team's success. You don't have to blow your own horn, simply tell everyone about the great things your team's doing and let them connect the dots."

Immerse Yourself in Smart People
"Some people are afraid to hire people who are smarter than they are. I believe just the opposite. If you treat people the way I do, you'll never be threatened by someone smarter than you. More importantly, if you immerse yourself in smart people, your team will perform better, they'll get even greater visibility and as the leader of a smart team, you'll be recognized as someone who can handle greater responsibility."

Pace Yourself, it's the Race of Your Lifetime
"The biggest mistake I see people make is to drive too hard for the almighty dollar. They push and push for promotions, raises, and bonuses every chance they get. It doesn't take much of this type of behavior to earn the wrong reputation. Today at IBM we are focused on those who demonstrate the ability to drive results across organizational boundaries. These individuals are the ones who are recognized with raises and bonuses. We're no longer paying just for great results; we now look beyond what was accomplished to how it was accomplished. I recently had to tell an employee who had overachieved 110 percent of their measureable goal that they would not be getting the performance review they were expecting. This person had achieved the numbers by working as a loner. They could have gotten better

results with less angst by taking a more collaborative approach. I had to make a point that their future at IBM, or anywhere for that matter, would be limited if they continued down this path."

"One of my greatest mentors was a fellow named Ralph Holt. He was a minor league pitcher for the Red Sox and my little league coach. I wanted to pitch more than anything else in baseball. Ralph appreciated that, but he also wanted me to be successful. He limited my pitching until I was ready at 12 years old. He was right. I turned out to be a pretty good pitcher and led my team to the New York State Little League finals twice. Ralph knew what I've since learned. Life is not a sprint, it's a marathon; your career, even more so. You can burn out so easily, it's unbelievable, but if you take a longer term view, pace yourself, and spend time developing the people you meet along the way, it's not that difficult to have a successful career without worrying about the next lay-off or missing your kids growing up because you had to work nights and weekends. It's just a matter of understanding how people work and finding the right balance."

Desperate Measures—Forcing A Raise

First of all, let me be very clear: forcing a raise from your boss is one of the most dangerous things you can do to your career. As we just discussed, companies have guidelines, pay grades, pay grids, and review cycles that are generally sacred. Trying to force your boss to break these corporate sacraments has a low probability of success, and tremendous downside. If your boss is a middle manager, he'll probably need to go up through several levels to get an exception approved. This means that your attempt to force a raise will be common knowledge in the upper echelons of the company. If your boss is a member of the upper echelon, he may fear his breaking the system will be viewed as a sign of weakness among his peers. More importantly, as soon as you try and force a raise, you threaten your relationship with your boss. If you succeed, you may get more than you bargained for. Yes, more money, but you'll also taint your reputation. You may become known as a malcontent, "not a team player", or simply someone who just cares about money. You will certainly be seen as impatient. Worse than that, if you fail to get the raise you think you deserve, you'll never look at your boss or even the company you work for the same way again. You'll feel unappreciated, your motivation will slip, and you'll invariably find yourself sniffing around for a new job.

Despite that severe warning, I still know that there will be times when you feel that you just need to force your boss to give you a raise. Here are some tips on how to improve your odds of success and limit your downside risks:

1. **Pick the Right Time to Make Your Move.** Forcing a raise is a little like card counting in blackjack. If you pay attention to what's going on around you and wait until the time is right to up your bet, you will dramatically reduce your risk of losing. When are the good times to try to force a raise? Certainly when you're on a roll. Right after a great performance, better yet, right after you pulled off something special that is above and beyond all expectations. Of course, this is pretty obvious and therefore nothing special. But unless you're performance is generally accepted as exceptional, don't even think about trying to force a raise.

2. **Have a Rock Solid Case.** The best example of this is when your boss brings in a senior person (with a senior salary) from outside the company, and they immediately bomb out. This type of mess can even put your boss's career at risk. But, if you can figure out how to step in and save the day, you're a hero and in the best possible position to win a promotion. Not only have you performed, but also you've proven that you are worthy of the same kind of money that your boss was willing to give the big shot from outside the company who just flamed out. Better yet, you also demonstrated that you are a true team player and capable of grace under fire by bailing your boss out of

a messy situation, without any complaining. This is the best situation to be in when you try to force a raise. Just be sure to wait until the smoke clears to make your move. Any hint that you're even thinking about money during the heat of battle will wipe out all of the potential good will and may even make your boss feel like you're holding him hostage.

3. **Graciously Set the Stage.** As important as the first two tips are, this is the most important ingredient to successfully forcing a raise. First of all, you cannot come across as trying to force anything. There can be no ultimatums, timelines, or threats. My favorite stage setter is, "I just feel underappreciated and I'm beginning to doubt myself in this job." Another one I used with great success is "I think you out-negotiated me when I took this job, if I knew X, Y, and Z before I accepted this job, I would have held out for more money or kept looking for a higher paying job elsewhere, "or simply": I feel like I'm trapped in an underpaying position." A lot of people will tell you that serious personnel matters should only be discussed face-to-face. I disagree. Whenever I get hit with a serious personnel matter face-to-face, I have an immediate reaction. If the person confronting me is sitting across the desk, it makes matters worse. I prefer to give and receive serious personnel matters in writing. This is not a good time for email, but rather a good old fashioned letter. My favorite is a handwritten note left on the boss's desk very, very early in the morning. For icing on the cake, you can even say "this situation has me so upset that I couldn't sleep last night, so I got up, and wrote you this letter."

4. **No Ultimatums**. You should not only avoid ultimatums, but actually bend over backwards to take any semblance of pressure off your boss. Conclude your letter or meeting by saying something like "I realize that you have bosses too and I don't expect you to rush out and fix this problem right away, but I felt compelled to let you know how I felt and hopefully you

can find a way to fix things before too long." The boss has no pressure; he may not even mention the situation to his boss or HR. But he will most likely feel badly about it and try to fix it as fast as possible. Even if he can't figure out a way, he'll be sure to bump you to the high end of the legal range at the next scheduled salary review.

This is exactly what I did after my unpleasant meeting with Marcellus about my missing retroactive raise. I went in to work the next day and asked Marcellus if he would mind if I met with his boss to "thank him for the raise." Of course, it took a few minutes to convince him that I wasn't going to shoot myself in the foot. When I got in front of the big guy and thanked him for the raise, he was truly blown away. He knew he had screwed me and he knew I knew it too. He never expected me to thank him. I made a great impression and turned the big boss into a career proponent in less than 15 minutes. Within a year, I got several more raises totaling 49 percent. I also resigned from inventory control to take a marketing job within the company. When Mars' boss heard about my resignation, he insisted on seeing me to try to change my mind. He laid out a plan to double my salary in the next 18 months. I graciously thanked him for his support, but I left and took the marketing job anyway.

You may have noticed that I've avoided any discussion of resignation as a way to force a raise. Threatening to resign as a way to force a raise is a fool's game. I've had a few people try it. In most cases, I may have actually given them the raise, but I instantly labeled them with my own form of the Scarlet Letter. I started planning the future without them and started limiting their responsibilities. If they had any subordinates, I went out of my way to get to know them. If I had any important new assignments to hand out, I gave them to others on the team. In short, I penciled them out of my long-term plans.

That said, you might be in the process of actually resigning—because you truly want to go somewhere else—

but find yourself faced with a very attractive counteroffer to stay. This has happened to me twice, but in both cases I declined and moved on. I take resigning very seriously and spend months making lists of reasons why I must resign before I even start looking for a new job. Once I have finished negotiating an attractive offer for a new job, I just go in and resign. I don't angle for a counteroffer—wild horses couldn't stop me from leaving. On those few occasions when people who worked for me resigned and I successfully turned them around and convinced them to stay, money was not the reason they were leaving. In order to turn them around I had to deal with their real issues first. But in every case, the new job offer paid more than they were making. In the end, I also had to match the offer they had in hand. In a way I succumbed to a forced raise, but I never thought of it that way. I believed they were leaving for bigger reasons and never gave the raise a second thought. Of course, if they ever tried it again, I'd smell a rat and just wish them well in their future. When it comes to resigning, never resign as a way to force a raise. If you resign, do so to move on to a better place. If you get a counteroffer, be gracious and always appear to give it serious consideration. But know that money will never fix the real problems and unless your boss will fix your real issues, you'll never be happy, no matter what they pay you.

Bank Your Raise

A recent study by the Creighton University Center for Marriage and Family found that the three biggest obstacles to satisfaction in the lives of newly married couples were balancing job and family, frequency of sexual relations, and debt brought into marriage. I'm certainly not going anywhere near sex in this book, but clearly the other two obstacles hit close to home. I know people who are considered very wealthy people and people who would be classified as the "working poor." I have seen people with huge incomes become miserable over money. I have also witnessed poor people enjoy life every day and always seem to have a little pocket money. There is an old axiom that goes: "It's not what you make, it's what you keep."

When it comes to how you internalize your salary, nothing could be more relevant. If you want to be miserable about money your entire life, get obsessed over your next raise and immediately increase your standard of living every time you get more money. If you want to eliminate the number one cause of stress in your life, bank your raise. By that I mean as soon as you get a raise, figure out how much more you'll be taking home every paycheck and automatically deposit that money into your bank account. It may sound corny, but save it for a rainy day—because there will be rainy days. Yes, getting a raise and getting promoted is a wonderful thing, but if it becomes your obsession, you'll wake up one day and find that you've missed a lot of your life and all you have to show for it is more stuff. Bank your raise; it will give you freedom to pursue more options and avoid one of the top sources of stress to you and your family.

CAREER Secret Sauce

STRATEGY EIGHT

Career Saving Moves

I sincerely hope that the readers of Career Secret Sauce never find themselves in deep career trouble, but statistically it will happen to virtually everyone:

- The Employment Policy Foundation says about one-quarter of all new hires won't make it through their first year.

- Leadership IQ, a training firm that studied 20,000 newly hired employees over three years, found that almost half (46 percent) of rookies wash out in the first 18 months.

- International HR consultants Development Dimensions reported that 53 percent of managers and executives brought on board from outside are gone within a year.

The first seven chapters of *Career Secret Sauce* have focused on ways to create a great career and steer clear of various on-the-job landmines. I truly believe that if you take these lessons to heart and apply them to your own situation, you'll never need Strategy Eight. But sometimes luck is out of your favor or a risk you took to get ahead blows up in your face and you find yourself hustling for survival. If that time comes, your first instinct will likely be to update your résumé and start looking for a new job. That's never a bad idea, but as we'll discuss in Strategy Nine: In Search of Greener Pastures, it's tough to find a great new job at the drop of a hat. It's even tougher when you're under pressure or taking a beating in your current job. Sometimes the best path to greener pastures requires a little patience to first survive your current job long enough for that perfect opportunity to come around. Strategy Eight: Career Saving Moves is all about techniques you can use to weather a sudden career storm, keep a paycheck coming, and most importantly, buy time until something you really want opens up. You may even discover that great opportunity you're seeking at your current employer—if you can survive the temporary tribulation.

Holy Cow—I'm In Deep Trouble

Life at work will always be full of ups and downs. One day you score a nice promotion and you feel like you're floating on cloud nine—you are invincible. Your career is finally on a winning trajectory that will carry you for years. Then you get into a losing argument with your boss about priorities, he treats you with disrespect and your self esteem plummets. You feel unappreciated and expendable; you probably start thinking about finding a new job. Life is an emotional roller coaster—why should work be any different? Over time, you become accustomed to this trend and get a little calloused about the severity of the dark moments. Then one day something really bad happens and it hits you: this one feels different. This time you think you could be in serious trouble. Panic sets in.

How do you recognize a true career threat from a simple down day? There are no simple rules for detection, but there are a few clues you should watch for, particularly if you see more than one rearing its ugly head at the same time:

- There is a significant downturn in your company's business performance

- Your boss gets fired or his responsibilities get cut back

- Your company's industry is in a slump and profits plummet

- Your responsibilities are cut back and/or transferred to others

- Your company is acquired and outside analysts mention "cost synergies"

- A former peer gets promoted and becomes your new boss

- Your company brings in a new executive from the outside to "shake things up"

- It's not your imagination; people start treating you like you no longer exist

You may have noticed that I've mixed things together in this list. There are macro factors involving your company or industry that are well out of your control. If you get laid off because of this sort of trouble, it's less likely to scar your résumé, but you'll still be missing a paycheck until you land another job. There are a number of signs that you may have stepped on (or near) a political landmine.

Of all of chapters in Career Secret Sauce, Strategy Eight: Career Saving Moves is the one that is most personal to me. For the first 15 years of my career, I made multiple missteps before realizing that I was my own worst enemy. That epiphany was ultimately the impetus that led to this book. I know all about career saving moves because I've had to invent plenty of them just to stay alive. For that reason, the beginning of this lesson will lean heavily on my own personal "Waterloos" to illustrate real world predicaments and the actual strategies I applied to survive. We will also look at ways to minimize the damage of termination or a layoff. Again, I hope you never have to use these techniques, but just in case, here they are.

Early Warning Signs Are Seldom Obvious

It was June, 1982 and I had been at Data Terminal Systems for over six years. I had already survived a number of close calls with trouble, but managed to land on my feet and eventually ascend to the level of director in the marketing department at the tender age of 29. My boss, Dr. David Carlson, had been sent on a temporary assignment to Italy to help a major partner get up to speed with our products. I was Dave's young protégé, but because of my age, it would have been inappropriate to make me the acting department vice president. Instead, he gave the assignment to a seasoned salesman who we'll call Buster. DTS was on the verge of a severe business downturn. Our largest competitors were finally closing the technology gap we'd been enjoying for almost a decade and orders were starting to slip. As an experienced sales guy, Buster was more in tune with the impending doom than I was. While Dave was out of the country, he went to the President with a drastic proposal to cut costs and among other things, recommended closing down my department and laying virtually everyone off. Desperate to minimize any losses, Warren Tyler—the President, welcomed the plan and told Buster to inform Dave in Italy. Dave returned to the US and avoided me for most of the first day. Around 6:00 p.m. he met with me and within five minutes I could tell things were serious. The tone of voice and the look in his eyes revealed that the situation was beyond his control and he too was in danger. In the past, we had always discussed our potential political moves with confidence. Now he was using terms like "I'll try" or "it's hard to predict." Three days later I was laid off along with most of my people. In retrospect, I should have realized that my close relationship with my boss was as much a liability as an asset. As long as he held power, I was probably safe, but my relationship also made me a target for Dave's adversaries who were afraid to attack him directly. Going after me was a safe way for Buster to test

Dave's power with Warren. Once he saw that Warren would do anything to cut costs, Buster knew that he could undermine Dave directly.

I should have seen it coming when Buster was put in charge and taken appropriate action to build a relationship with him. The four months of unemployment that followed were painful and frightening. The emotional scars that were left behind helped me to develop a keen sense of potential danger. Although I dodged a number of bullets since 1982, and I was never fired, or even laid off again. Here are four personal tales of potential woe and the steps I took to craft a "happy ending".

The Best Shelter In A Storm—Take A Job Nobody Wants

Four months after being laid off at DTS, I landed a nice job at Prime and proceeded to move up the ladder rather smartly. By March of 1984, I had regained my director's title, only this time it was a much larger company. In my November 1985 performance review, my boss Chuck Reilly gave me very high marks and even listed "promotion to vice president" as my next career move.

Thirty days later, Chuck was promoted and given responsibility over multiple adjacent departments. His new position included leadership over groups that had previously been political adversaries. In an effort to smooth the political waters, Roy Brubaker, Chuck's boss, leaned on Chuck to give his old job to the most antagonistic members of the rival department, a fellow we'll call Adam. Although Adam clashed with everyone in our group, he and I shared the most contentious relationship. Within thirty days he had managed to slash my year-end bonus to the bone and turn my people against me. He also redefined the measurement system for my job and gave me quantitative goals that were humanly impossible. It was clear that I was being set up for the dreaded "termination with cause."

161

My Career Saving Move: In an effort to avoid another firing, I volunteered to step down and take the job of Director Commercial Industry Marketing, reporting to the strongest of Adam's peers, John Rockman. The job had been empty for a while and would have been forgotten if I hadn't volunteered to take it. Unlike Adam, John was a director-level manager like me; he aspired to become a vice president, didn't care for Adam, and was probably upset that he hadn't been named to the next Vice President post. I knew John would think that having a director report to him would strengthen his case for promotion to vice president. John wasn't really that popular of a boss either and most of his other direct reports were pretty junior. People thought I was crazy to volunteer to go from reporting to a Vice President to working for John, but I was in real trouble. My wife was pregnant with Natalie and the local job market was soft. Rather than trust my career to a man I knew was out to get me, I swallowed my pride and made John a very happy man.

All this move did was buy time. I quickly went to work on moving forward again and discovered a major business opportunity for Prime in Europe. Within twelve months, I was promoted to Managing Director for the Banking Technology Centre in London and back to reporting directly to Chuck. When I returned to the states, both Adam and John had left the company and I was able to start rebuilding the career that had almost fallen apart. Although I spent close to a year in corporate purgatory, I managed to retain my director's title and keep my foreign-service salary adjustment; effectively ending up with a 25 percent pay raise. Not bad for returning from the brink of disaster.

Sometimes You Have To Go Backwards To Move Forward

In 1988, Benet LeBow led a group of "corporate raiders" in an attempted hostile takeover of Prime. These guys made their money issuing junk bonds to raise cash for the acquisition and then breaking up the company into pieces and paying themselves a multi-million dollar management fee. Within days of the takeover attempt, everyone between me and the Chairman of Board was either fired or sent into early retirement. Prime had recently acquired Computervision and was in the process of redefining itself as a Computer Aided Design (CAD) vendor. I ran marketing for the banking industry and it was obvious that the company planned to downsize everything that didn't directly serve the CAD market. They replaced our benevolent CEO Joe Henson with an ex-GE guy named Tony Craig who earned his reputation slashing payrolls at General Electric. Suddenly I was at great risk again. Steve Fisch, the vice president who replaced Chuck Reilly, had initially told me that I'd "be safe." Then one week before the dreaded layoff day, he told me that my reputation was too tainted and he was going to "have to let me go."

My Career Saving Move: I only had a week to act, so the first thing I did was to figure out if anyone in the company had any job openings. There were only three, but they all required experience in CAD, something I didn't have. I met with the hiring executives for the first two job openings and left unimpressed. Not only were the jobs uninteresting, but the people I'd be reporting to were obviously going nowhere. Eventually I met Jim Meagher, a very well connected director with a long history at Computervision. Jim offered me a manager-level job that would require me to give up my director's title. The job was in the sales department, which generally pays better than marketing, so I would not have to take a pay cut. Ultimately, it was a fun job and I learned a lot about sales along the way. The experience literally turned my career around, and got me started on the road to developing Career Secret Sauce. Working for Jim gave me a new career trajectory that ultimately led to my position as head of worldwide marketing operations for the entire company in 1993. Had I been unwilling to take a step backward and surrender my senior job title, I never would have been able to move forward.

The Boldest Move—Relocate

As I mentioned earlier, one of the keys to my career saving move under the torment of Adam involved a temporary relocation to London. Relocations cost companies a lot of money and generally they are tied to trying to fill a job no one else will take.

In 1990, I had a relatively secure job with a bleak future. My superstar boss (Jim Meagher) had moved on and I was now reporting to a lackluster former peer. I provided corporate sales leadership for major national accounts like Martin Marietta, Hughes, and Rockwell. Because most of the action happened on the west coast, I developed a close relationship with the Regional Director, Steve Saucy. The western region always struggled to meet their sales goals, and the worst area of all was the northwest district. In the first quarter of 1990, it only achieved 18 percent of plan. The situation got so bad that after the quarter was over, the District Manager, Sam Lawrence, actually volunteered to be laid off from the company. No one wanted his job and the company was having a tough time even finding someone to interview. In addition to my stagnant job situation, I lived in Massachusetts and witnessed the worst housing value meltdown in history. Home prices dropped over one percent per month and at that point in time, my home equity represented my entire net worth.

My Career Saving Move: I approached Saucy at a social event in San Diego, California and delicately expressed some interest in replacing Sam as the Northwest District Manager. I had virtually no sales experience and thus would never have been considered for a district manager's position in a healthy territory. Unlike a career sales manager, my downside of failure would be minimal; expectations for a sales turnaround were low and anything above 18 percent of goal would be deemed a success. If all else failed, I could return to marketing with enhanced qualifications thanks to my stint in real sales. Saucy aggressively recruited me to fill the position and since no one else wanted the job, I negotiated a guaranteed salary for the first six months and got the company to buy my house in Massachusetts for 20 percent above the market price. We also got a fat relocation package and ended up in sunny Pleasanton, California on someone else's nickel and bought a new house at the beginning of one of those famous California housing booms.

Things actually turned out even better. The poor sales performance in 1990 resulted in pent-up demand in 1991. Coupled with the very modest sales goal I had negotiated, the northwest district achieved 148 percent of goal in that year. They named me Sales Manager of the Year, transferred me back to marketing in Massachusetts in 1992, and promoted me to senior marketing manager for North America.

Doing Nothing Can Be The Best Move

As you may have observed, my career saving moves got bolder and more creative as my career progressed. Back in 1977, at the very beginning of my career, I actually stumbled into the biggest mess of my life and lived to tell about it.

I was working in the materials department at Data Terminal Systems. There was an opening in marketing for manager of sales administration. I was anxious to move up the ladder and make more money. I had also concluded that the action was in marketing, not materials and even though this wasn't a true marketing job, it would be a foot in the door and certainly pay more. The hiring manager (we'll call him Len) seemed glad that I applied and made me very comfortable in the interview. He gave me a verbal offer and I went back to my boss in materials and asked for permission to transfer. They fought hard, but ultimately I won out. I probably burned a few bridges, but I wanted the new job. Everything was going well until the first day. About an hour after I started, a memo came out announcing my new position. There was only one problem: *it wasn't the job I had applied for, nor was it a job I wanted!* To make matters worse, the memo didn't go out under Len's name; it went out under the name of a guy

165

named Mark who reported to Len. I had never interviewed with Mark and I had fully expected to have him reporting to me. Len had been completely dishonest with me and now I was stuck in a job I didn't want, reporting to a guy I didn't respect, in a department that I now know was run by a man with zero integrity.

My Career Saving Move: I initially ran to Human Resources and Len's boss to file confidential complaints, but it was a small company and no one wanted to mess with Len. He was very active in office politics and everyone assured me that I'd lose any fight I picked with him. There were no viable solutions to my problem. I couldn't go back to my old job and they weren't about to force Len to make a management change he didn't want to do. I had 18 months of experience in Materials Management and that wasn't going to be enough to get a decent job anywhere else. So, I just stuck it out.

It turned out that Len was gunning for Mark and within a month Mark was gone and I had his job. A few months later, I caught a real break. Len brought a guy we'll call Kent to fill the job I thought I had been offered. Kent turned out to be a complete buffoon. I started cleaning up his messes and within one year of being shafted by Len, I was promoted into the job I originally wanted; replacing Kent, who had been canned by Len. Although I never trusted Len, we did develop a good relationship over the years. In particular, once he saw that I could "take a punch," he trusted me with increased responsibilities. By 1980, I managed a complex group of departments with over 30 subordinates. All I did to make it happen was turn the other cheek after being slapped in the face by a man with no integrity. Doing nothing was the right move.

Layoff Survival Techniques

The four scenarios described above were all successful in helping me to avoid my second layoff and actually set the stage for continued career advancement. The pain associated with my 1982 layoff gave me the motivation to do whatever it took to avoid ever letting it happen again.

That layoff came at a pretty bad time. We had just moved into our first house and taken on our first mortgage. I remember doing a budget just before I lost my job and we only had $50 a week left over for food and clothing! We were in deep trouble if I didn't find a job quickly.

Because my old boss, Dave Carlson, felt badly about my sudden termination, I had someone still inside the company to negotiate with. I was able to secure up to four and a half months of continued salary and benefits provided that I notified the company if I found work, at which everything would cease. I was able to get another job in two months that paid 20 percent more money. More importantly, I avoided getting close to running out of money.

In most cases, it is very difficult to negotiate severance terms following a company-wide layoff. Employment Law dictates that everyone be treated the same. This is not the case if you're being fired for cause. Companies fear wrongful dismissal lawsuits and will generally grant additional severance benefits in exchange for a "release." In most cases, companies offer layoff packages that continue benefits longer for employees who have been with the company the longest. A typical formula might be two weeks for everyone and an additional two weeks for every year of service. This would translate into a three month severance package for an employee with five years of tenure. Although the terms associated with a layoff are relatively fixed, you can still employ a number of winning strategies to minimize the damage.

Forestall Departure Through Interim Employment

A common reaction to news of your own layoff is immediately protesting and trying to reverse it. People often plead for their old job, reveal sorted details about the personal hardship they'll suffer, and sometimes even argue that another employee should be terminated in their place. None of these techniques ever work. The only reasonable reaction to being told that you're being laid off is to behave rationally. It is vital for you to convince your former supervisor that you understand the predicament and that you still care about his welfare and that of the company. At the very least, this will earn you a future job reference and an ally in your job search. Better yet, it could also set the stage for something even more valuable—interim employment.

It is a lot tougher to find a new job when you're unemployed than when you're working. People naturally assume that you're out of work for a reason. Therefore, once you learn that you're being laid off, you should do everything possible to create the illusion that you're still employed.

Once your boss is convinced that you fully accept your fate, and care only for the future welfare of the company, he's ready to listen to your ideas about how you can help him avoid a problem by coming back to help wrap things up. The key is to secure access to the facilities, retain a phone number at the company, and engage in some work that you can report to a potential employer as honest work. Sometimes you can get paid for this and sometimes you can't. The point is to develop a situation where you can truthfully say "I'm still with them, but they know I'm leaving."

The specific proposals for staying on vary by discipline. Finance and HR people have the most legitimate claim on interim employment, just to clean up the mess. But there are other good strategies. Companies fear upsetting customers by terminating salespeople. If you're a sales person being laid off, you can propose a 30-day project to transition account knowledge to your replacement and offer to "smooth the waters" with the customer. In the case of technical people like engineers or computer specialists, companies fear losing intellectual property and will often pay extra to make sure all of your project know-how is documented and passed on to others. Think of all the ways you can help the company quickly absorb your absence, and then come up with a short-term proposal to do it for them. Remember, your old job is gone, so don't assume your old pay grade. Staying on the old company payroll for one day a week for two more months is much better than getting one extra 40-hour week paycheck.

Look Busy

Even if you do land interim work with your former employer, you may still run out of time before you find your next job. This doesn't mean you have to surrender and march around wearing the Scarlet Letter of "unemployed." It just means you have to find something to keep you busy that will look legitimate on your résumé. I'm not talking about a temporary job with your brother-in-law painting houses or volunteer work for your church (although I highly recommend it). I'm talking about doing something that will make you more valuable in the eyes of a potential employer; for example:

Help a small company—Talk to friends and relatives to try to locate someone who has a small company that could use your skills. Offer to help them for free (of course, you can take money if they offer). You may find someone who is in pure start-up mode seeking funding. There will be plenty to do, just no money. At least you'll have a "current" job listed on your résumé that could possibly turn into a real job.

Consult—Approach your former employer's competitors, suppliers, or customers and engage them in a discussion about how your experience can be of service. If you can't win a paying assignment, offer to work for free on a probationary basis. Make it clear that they have no obligation to ever hire you and that you may leave with little notice if you get a real job offer. You'd be surprised how many people respond favorably to this kind of creativity.

Start a Book—Everyone has a book inside them. You have expert knowledge in your vocation; think about how you'd teach what you know to others and begin writing it down. It will keep your skills sharp and give you a winning entry on your résumé —"author." Imagine sitting in an interview

169

and having a perspective employer ask you about the book you're writing. You'll surely impress him with your expertise!

Leverage The Second Network

Obviously, you'll want to immediately hit your primary personal network to locate any referral job opportunities you can. We'll spend a lot of time discussing this in Strategy Nine. But there is a second network that you shouldn't overlook; the network of other people who were laid off at the same time. These may be people you were never close to at work. They may also be people you hope to never meet again. But for now, they represent a valuable asset in your arsenal of career saving moves. A dialogue with this network can provide a lot of important intelligence:

- Did any of the other layoff victims get a special deal?

- Did any of them get interim work?

- Which companies in your region or industry are hiring?

- Who has already found work and are there additional opportunities?

- Does anyone have a good strategy for staying busy until a real job comes along?

- Does anyone want to start a company?

Never Forget The Pain

We are on this earth for various and mysterious reasons, but one of them is to work. Unemployment is not only painful, it's unnatural. When it strikes, you can follow the lessons we've covered here to minimize the damage to your career. The most important lesson is to never forget the pain; channel it to fuel your early warning senses, perseverance in the face of doom, and creativity in finding a new opportunity with greater security.

Profile Mike Sandler
Even a Good Guy Can Get In Trouble

Before I met Mike in 2006, all I knew about him was that he was actor Adam Sandler's "Uncle Mike." I have always loved Adam's work so I was predisposed to liking Mike before I ever met him. The funny thing is the more I got to know him the more I liked him. In fact, he's one of the most likable guys I've ever met; and that's a big part of his story.

Mike began his career in New York City cold calling chemical companies and pitching out-of-work chemical engineers; a placement agent. One day he said to himself "if I can find great jobs for these clowns I can probably find myself a better job."

Mike was always a sharp dresser; at 6'6" tall he enjoys dressing well and fine clothing. He had figured out that his career happiness would be best served by doing what he enjoyed so he pulled out the Yellow Pages and started cold calling fashion companies and pitching himself. Eventually he caught a break and got a job with Eagle Clothing as an apprentice. After two years of hauling inventory, cleaning up other people's messes, and filing, he got his first shot as a salesman. Although Mike worked for Eagle for 7 years from the day he started until the day he left they called him "Rookie."

The fashion industry in NY is a tight community of intertwined businesses. Clothing companies sell to retailers, they license design categories from famous designers and produce full collections based on those designs. Eagle Clothes grew to become one of the largest and most successful clothing companies, so when Eagle went under after trying to expand from manufacturing into retail, Mike was well positioned to land another job. Mike's career path progressed from sales to general management. He worked in a variety of companies; both large and small. He saw fantastic growth years and had his share of disappointments.

171

Mike's rich experience working in a very tough industry made him an expert in career saving moves. I asked him to share some of the lessons he learned along the way.

The truth isn't always the best thing "After a couple of years of dog work at Eagle, I finally got a chance to sell. I was so nervous on my first sales call that I told the customer it was my first day selling and I was scared to death that I'd end up a failure. He felt so sorry for me that he gave me a big order. That line worked so well that I used it with every new customer I met for the first 6 months and boy did I sell a lot of clothes."

Trouble Just Happens "When I was 39 one of my clothing manufacturers in South America asked me to come to work for them and set up a US company. It was the first time I had the title president after my name and it was a big deal for me. I worked my tail off and spent a ton of personal equity leaning on old customers to order this stuff. I traveled to Bogota, got wined and dined by the family and thought I was really on to something big. They never delivered a quality product and couldn't keep a production schedule. One day the owner walked into my office and said "give me the keys to the Porsche." They went out of business within the next twelve months."

"I was really shook up. I took the summer off and tried to figure out how I could be so stupid. I finally realized that stuff like this just happens; it doesn't mean you're a failure. You just have to have confidence in yourself and you'll get through it. Before I knew it, I landed a new job and my career was back on a winning track."

Most Jerks Get Their Just Deserts "Right after the Columbian debacle I got a call from a guy I'd worked with years ago. He asked me to join him at The Greif Companies. They licensed Perry Ellis, Polo, Chaps, Lanvin of Paris and other top brands. Most importantly, they were owned by Genesco Corporation; a billion dollar public company. I had a nice run with Greif, the product line grew to over one hundred million in annual sales in the six years we ran it. Then things changed. Genesco recruited a new president out of Proctor and Gamble to shake things up. The new President called me and my boss Norman to a meeting in Atlanta to discuss his style, philosophy, and business goals. At the end I said to Norman that I thought the meeting went pretty well, but he just looked at me and said "it's over." Norman knew what I was about to learn. This guy didn't know jack about the fashion business."

"A few weeks later, I was in a meeting with the new President and he was espousing his new strategy for a massive inventory expansion. I stood up, looked him the eye and said "this ain't Tide; that idea won't work." The guy said nothing; he just took a pen and made a note to himself. Weeks later I was gone."

"Shortly after that the guy from P&G was named Chairman of the Board. He started making lots of radical changes that might have worked in the soap business, but were suicidal in the clothing industry. Within a year, Greif went down the tubes and the guy was fired."

If Something Stinks, It's Probably Rotten "Right after Greif, a designer named Robert Stock asked me to join up with him and sell his designs all over the world. Things seemed to be going well and then one day he tells me there isn't enough money coming in to the company to pay both of us. I was running sales, licensing, design and marketing and I knew this wasn't true—there was plenty of money. Anyway, we parted company. I later found out that his accountant was robbing him blind. I just knew something was wrong."

Don't Expect Perfect Management "In 1992 I returned to Biderman Industries, a company I had worked for earlier in my career. The company was in trouble and Maurice Biderman, the owner, asked me to come in and help get things back on track. I was the President of the Yves St. Laurent Clothing Division and my peer was a woman, Jean, who was the President of the Dress Shirt and Sportswear

Division. Because of the mess they were in they had outside consultants everywhere looking for ways to get rid of people and cut costs. They asked me and Jean for our thoughts on how to save the company and we told them. One day Maurice and the consultants came to me and told me they were going to go with Jean's ideas and that I was going to be reporting to her! I told them to forget it; I quit. It was a dumb idea and I expected more out of Maurice."

Make Friends Along the Way "I never felt like my career was in serious trouble. My old mentor Norman was also a good friend and whenever he turned something up he called me to see if I was interested. I made good friends with my customers and suppliers and they were always there when I needed help.

Take the Good People with you "I spent the last fifteen years at Lanier Clothes, a division of Oxford Industries a public company; they licensed Nautica, Oscar De La Renta, and Geoffrey Beene. As President of these divisions, I had the ability to hire a lot of people. I did the same thing my mentor Norman did for me. I filled most of the key jobs with people I'd met along the way. With the help of all these people, Lanier grew to $175 million in annual sales and extremely profitable. You just can't make enough friends along the way. They are the real secret to job security."

STRATEGY NINE

In Search Of Greener Pastures

It's time to go.

I don't mean running out the door because your boss wasn't nice to you, your raise was smaller than everyone else's, or your new cubicle faces the men's room door. Eventually, it's just time for a change.

How do you know when the time is right? There is no simple answer. Over the course of my career, my tenure and reason for leaving varied widely:

Employer	Tenure	Rationale
DTS	7 Years	Laid off
Prime/CV	10 Years	Resigned to get away
Concentra	2 Years	Resigned for a better opportunity
Aspect/i2	7 Years	Resigned to get away
XPORTA	2 Years	Sold off the company

Of all of these, probably the most painless was getting laid off. Sure, I was nervous at first, but I had a small severance package and found a new job before it ran out; but unlike every other job change, it didn't involve any deep decision-making on my part.

On the other hand, in each of the other cases—where I initiated the resignation—it was hell. I experienced guilt, fear, second-guessing, and the loss of good friends. Yet looking back, I have to say that I never left a job too soon and I never regretted moving on when I did.

Some people say you have to stay at least 5 years or your résumé looks fishy. I don't believe in such simplistic rules of thumb; there are very few hiring managers that will give someone with a string of 2-year stints a second look, and many hiring managers fear that a candidate who's been in the same job for 10-15 years may have difficulty adjusting.

There are some key indicators that it's the right time (or wrong time) to search for greener pastures. Leaving a job too soon or taking the wrong job in haste is probably the second biggest mistake you make in your life (I think marrying the wrong person is probably number one). That's why Strategy Nine: In Search of Greener Pastures is the final lesson in Career Secret Sauce.

I once worked for a guy named Chuck Reilly who was a Master Machiavellian. Like the medieval prince, he trusted no one, always looked out for himself, and was so effective at manipulating people they often never knew it was happening. He once told me, "leaving your job is a three-step process and you must never let these steps get out of order."

I hate to admit it, but I think Chuck was right!

Step One: Convince yourself that it is time to leave your current employer, independent of any new job opportunity that might be on the horizon. Specifically, you must have exhausted all internal job transfers that might help you advance your career with your current employer, improve your reputation, or fix whatever else is bothering you. Simply having a lousy boss or job situation is not enough if there are transfer opportunities available elsewhere in the company.

Step Two: Convince yourself that the company you are going to is the right one for you. In the late nineties, I was working for Aspect Development when we missed a quarter. The stocked dropped to $6/share and many weak hearts hit the streets and went to work for sexy young Internet companies. Within a year, Aspect recovered and the stock went up over $200 per share. Most of the Internet companies the weaklings had run off to had peaked and ultimately collapsed. They made the mistake of looking at Aspect too critically and looking at glitzy Internet companies through rose colored glasses. Do your homework on the market and financial condition of any company you're thinking about going to and then do it again!

The key ingredient for success is the work environment. Go back and reread Strategy Two: Select An Employer That Suits Your Nature. Talk to people in the new company other than the hiring manager and personnel department. Try to profile the environment you'll be working in and make sure it suits your nature.

Step Three: Convince yourself that the specific job you're going to is the right one for you. It may well be time for you to move on and you've picked the right company, but the job you're considering is all wrong. This is one of the easiest ways to "jump from the frying pan into the fire." If the job is beneath you, it may take years to catch up to where you belong. If the job is too big, you'll crash and burn before you know it—then what? Take a good, hard look at your potential new boss. Is he or she obviously more senior than you are, or someone you could imagine as your peer or even a subordinate? If it's the latter, you may be taking a job that's beneath you. Just because the new job pays more doesn't mean it's a logical step upward in your career.

Similarly, take the time to understand the goals and objectives you're signing up for in the new job. If you aren't comfortable with your ability to achieve the results expected, you may be making a serious career mistake.

The operative word here is CAUTION. Most likely you'll only make three to five company moves in your life. Make certain you're doing them for the right reasons and your chances for success will be much better.

Reasons For Leaving; The Good, Bad, And Ugly

As I said in the outset, and in career saving moves, the worst reason for leaving is a reaction to something petty, painful, or emotional on the job. The three I mentioned, "your boss was mean to you, your raise was too small, or you don't like your new office space" are probably the most common wrong reasons for leaving. The other popular ones are, "someone else (besides me) got the promotion," "I don't like my new boss," or "I'm worried about a layoff." Of these six, the last one is probably the only valid one in the bunch; assuming the layoff concern is valid.

Beyond impending financial doom, the other two good reasons for hitting the road are (1) "I've gone as far as I can go in this company," and (2) "my reputation here is tarnished beyond repair." Unfortunately, when your image is shot inside your current employer, it's likely to be discovered by anyone who's thinking about hiring you. Most good companies go beyond the references you provide when checking out a potential new hire. If you decide it's time to move on because of your damaged reputation, you may need to spend six to twelve months doing repair work before you can safely withstand a rigorous reference check (see Strategy Eight: Career Saving Moves for more details).

If you pay attention to what's happening around you, it's easy to figure out when your employer is hitting the wall. Even before the layoff begins, there are early warning signs. Typically lost orders, disappointing sales results or widespread cost-cutting programs signal impending trouble. You may be able to stack up accomplishments by saving a company that's going downhill, but they won't have the same glitter on your résumé that growth-oriented ones have. Shutting down an unprofitable plant or product line, creating a new and highly restricted travel policy, or taking over your former coworker's responsibilities after they have all moved on certainly feel like accomplishments when you're in the heat of battle, but viewed from the outside world, they look like acts of desperation on a sinking ship. In almost every case, your career will benefit more if you are the first to see trouble on the horizon and take action to protect yourself than it will from hanging around doing a superb job cleaning up the mess.

While it's pretty easy to deduce that your employer is about to hit the rocks, it's a lot tougher to conclude that your opportunities for advancement are truly tapped; it's just too subjective. If, after a string of promotions, things slow down, look around. Where is your next real promotion going to come from? Can you do your boss' job better than he can; is he going anywhere soon, how about his peers? If your only potential promotions involve someone resigning, getting fired or dropping dead, it may be time to start looking elsewhere.

It's also possible that you've moved up so fast that people can't see beyond your rookie image. It's just human nature to find it hard to envision the girl who processed invoices last year as the director of accounting this year, no matter how smart she is. But if you're that good, you owe it to yourself to keep moving.

There are good compensation reasons for moving on. If you made the mistake of coming into your current job at too low a salary, or just started at the wrong job level, you may be stuck inside the grid (see Strategy Seven: Promotionology; The Art of the Raise for more details). It's far easier for a new employer to pay you what you're worth than for your current one to give you a huge raise— even if it's less than they'll have to pay your replacement. Of course, your old boss may be able to match an offer from the outside and sail past mountains of red tape to keep you from walking away. I would never look for a new job with that outcome in mind, nor would I tear up an outside offer and go back to my old job just because they matched the money. I do know people who have come back for a matching offer and lived happily ever after, but there's more to life than money.

Finally, the best time to look for a new job is right after you've hit a personal home run. This may feel very counterintuitive: your boss finally loves you, your peers admire you, and your sense of job security has never been stronger, but this is the time to act. My father used to say, "Get off the stage while they're still applauding". Think about it. You'll have plenty of fresh accomplishments to wax on about as you interview and if things progress to reference checking, your odds of getting glowing referrals from former coworkers are high. Most importantly, your deep sense of self-confidence will show in every interview you give.

Changing jobs is like a six-month root canal. First there are two months of angst as you talk yourself into action; another two months of sneaking around to interview, enduring rejection, the heartache of actually turning in your resignation, rejecting counteroffers; and finally two months of being the "new guy" on the new job and not knowing how to do anything. This is not something you want to do very often. Ideally, four to five changes per career is about right. This means you need to land the best opportunity possible when you do move. In order to do so, you need to get a shot at every good opportunity that's out there.

Let's Talk Résumé

Before you can smoke out an opportunity, you must be ready to sell yourself as a terrific potential employee. This requires a great résumé. At the highest level, there are two schools of thought on résumés. The conventional wisdom is to have a very brief one- or two-pager, with just the bare facts. The other approach is to write a short story about your career, complete with accomplishments and all sorts of pertinent company or organizational information.

180

Executive search firms actually use both. They send out a stack of one to two pages to demonstrate to their clients how deep their talent pool is and once the client "shortlists" a few candidates, they get to look at the short story version.

The concept behind the one- to two-pager is to titillate the client and raise questions about the details behind the skimpy facts you've outlined. Hopefully you'll create enough curiosity to land an interview. While I see the logic in this approach, I have always preferred the second approach: write a short story about what you've actually accomplished in every job you've held.

It does take a lot more time to write an in-depth résumé that discusses past job goals, scope, and key accomplishments. It also takes time for someone else to read it. But in either case, the time is less than it takes for two people to have a meaningful interview. To me, the goal of the "short story résumé" is to overwhelm the potential employer with your capabilities and effectively eliminate the first interview. Also, since the ideal source of job opportunities is through some kind of referral, you don't need to waste time building curiosity.

Here is an excerpt from my "short story" résumé for a pretty brief stint in 1993:

COMPUTERVISION
Manager, North American Marketing
(January 1993 to December 1993)
- Senior marketing executive for North American Operations
- Managed two product managers, a marketing communications manager with a staff of 5 and an operating budget of $1.3 million.

Accomplishments:
- Created and launched new sales and marketing methodology that assessed the strategic drivers behind the customer's product development process and aligned our products and services with specific organizational productivity improvement programs at the enterprise level.

181

- Created and deployed a new company image program, positioning Computervision's downsizing as part of a strategic corporate reengineering.
- Created and launched "The Innovation Series." A business development program reaching over 800 executives and engineering professionals in 1993.
- Led team of 160 sales and marketing personnel on the floor at Autofact and earned the award for "The Most Promising Company of the Future" (30 days after announcing a $515 million loss—the largest loss in the history of our industry).
- The above programs drove revenue growth of 15% in the second half of 1993, reversing a first half decline.
- Named "Most Valuable Leader" in North America for 1993

Note the direct verbs used to describe my accomplishments: "created, launched, deployed, led, drove," and my favorite, "named."

This kind of deep résumé may not be appropriate for everyone. It may sound like puffery if you have a weak background or you're light on experience or measurable accomplishments. I would not use this style résumé to respond to a help wanted ad; it will simply irritate the screener who doesn't have time to read your epistle. That would be the situation for building curiosity.

The nice thing about the short story approach is that it's very easy to update. You simply add a new section in the beginning for your current job and take a look at the end to see if a position in the distant past can be condensed.

Regardless which style you choose, keep in mind that your résumé is a written abbreviation of you. Not only does every nuance speak volumes, it's the only thing doing the talking! Thus, your résumé can never be too perfect. Every detail—the layout, the font, your word choice—says something about you to a potential employer.

Career Secret Sauce is not a handbook on résumé writing; I just want to share tips that you might not find elsewhere. In general, any clean résumé that sticks to the facts has a

182

good chance of being read by a screener, but it's also not that hard to create a résumé that will virtually kill any chance you have of being called in for an interview.

Here is my personal Top 5 list of Résumé Blunders.

1. **Errors**—I have read thousands of résumés and about twenty percent of them have some kind of error. There is simply no excuse for making a typographical or grammatical mistake on your résumé, other than laziness or sloppiness. Most résumé screeners make their first pass looking for obvious candidates to reject. No one will waste their time interviewing a candidate who's so careless with something so important. Make certain your résumé is error free. Ask two or three friends to proofread it, and then do it again.

2. **Superfluous Creativity**—The format for a résumé is pretty well-established. You list the jobs you've held in reverse chronological order. Include your title, start and stop dates by year and month, then key accomplishments. There is an education section listing colleges, degrees, and dates of matriculation. If you're just starting your career, you may place your education at the top of page one, but after a few jobs, move it to the back. I've seen a number of candidates try and demonstrate how creative they are by inventing a new format for their résumé and it almost never works. They use job skills or some other attribute as their major résumé category and then mention jobs they've head as a secondary category. Another format mistake is to spend a lot of time waxing on about your job objective. Your job objective is to get a job! The only thing that a statement about objectives does is to force the screener to read it and conclude that your objectives don't meet their job opening. You will not get credit for creativity! Most likely the screener will get irritated and that's end of your job opportunity.

3. **Describing Responsibilities (instead of accomplishments)**—The résumé serves only one purpose; to make you stand out from other candidates and win an interview. How do you impress someone by telling them what you were responsible for without telling them how well you lived up to that responsibility? Hiring managers want to see what you've accomplished.

4. **Vague Results**—Accomplishments are good, but measurable results are better. Whenever possible, use numbers to back up your accomplishments. It's easy to report numbers if you're in sales or production, but what if you're in a support or creative role? If you think about it, you can find a numerical way to report virtually every accomplishment. Engineers can reference a reduction in design cycle time or improved product performance. Finance people can cite productivity improvements. Customer Service personnel can list improvements in survey results. When I was in marketing, we tracked the number of times our company was mentioned in the press. You can bet those numbers made it into my résumé.

5. **Too Much Personal Information**—For some strange reason, most people like to include a "Personal" section in their résumé and fill it with things that can only come back to haunt them. You may be proud of your five kids, but the screener may see that as a reason why you won't be willing to work late. Singing in the church choir or serving a local charity is very commendable, but an atheist or workaholic hiring manager could see them as an excuse not to hire you. Generally anything about outside hobbies or sports will always do more harm than good. Physical data is the most ridiculous thing you can list in résumé, yet people persist in listing their height, weight, and even age. I recommend that you skip the personal section of your résumé.

Where Are All Those Opportunities?

Although I only worked for five companies, I considered changing jobs on an almost annual basis. Over the years, I encountered four types of opportunities. First, there were job openings that I read about, sent in my résumé, and essentially applied for blind. The second source of job leads came from headhunters, or executive search firms. The third source came to my attention as a result of others referring me to someone I didn't know who was willing to give me a chance because of their relationship with the referrer. Finally, there were opportunities where someone I once worked for (or with) invited me to join them in a new company or department. Of these four, the best by far was the last one, especially when the person bringing me along was a rising star.

I never got a job, or even an interview by responding to a help wanted ad, so if that's a path you wish to pursue, you're on your own. However, I do know a lot about the other three and how to make them work to your advantage so that you always have a pool of new job opportunities waiting in the wings should you need them.

The Headhunter Game

The first headhunter to actually find me a job was Ron LaLiberte. The job was with Prime Computer and the guy who hired me—Paul Ardito—actually showed me a copy of my résumé where he had written in the word "NO" and then scratched it out. The reason he scratched it out and hired me was because Ron told him I was the best guy for the job. The reason Ron pushed me was because of my wife. She was at another company and her boss was hiring a lot of salespeople. Ron developed a relationship with her to gain access to her boss. When I was looking for a job, Ron returned the favor and effectively "placed me" at Prime Computer.

Once I saw the power Ron LaLiberte had to help me land a job, I made it my business to become "the best friend a headhunter could have." I did this by seizing every opportunity I could to make their job easier.

Headhunters have tough jobs. They need to find clients and candidates then persuade both of them that there's a match. They also have to constantly replenish their pool of qualified candidates and win new clients.

There are two types of headhunters; contingent and retained search. Contingent headhunters get paid only if you get hired. Retained search firms are hired exclusively by the employer and are responsible for finding and presenting the best available candidates for hire.

The contingent guys are generally worthless. They collect résumés, strip off the candidates contact information and then blast stacks of résumés to anyone who might be looking to hire. Not only does this reduce you to a piece of paper among similar pieces of paper, but it also means that an employer will have to "pay a ransom" of 20 percent of your first year's salary to hire you. Although Ron was a contingent guy, his relationship with Paul made him effectively retained; Paul used him exclusively and trusted his judgment.

A great relationship with a retained guy can be priceless if they have a search that matches your career aspirations. They have the best jobs and they are the gatekeeper. No one is likely to be considered who doesn't come through them, and their personal recommendation usually holds a great deal of weight. Unfortunately, they only do a few searches at a time and chances that their working on one that you qualify for are slim. I developed relationships with as many retained search firms as possible and thus I was always called when a good job in my industry opened up.

Although I was seldom looking for a new job, I always greeted a searching headhunter like an old lost friend. I would let him wax on about the employer, then I would ask a few of poignant questions about the position and generally conclude by saying, "I'm doing really well where I am, but give me a few days and I'll get back to you with some candidates." Then I always followed through and gave them some good names.

Frequently, the people I suggested made the shortlist; on a number of occasions they even got the job. After a few years of this, every headhunter I had ever talked to called me as soon as they got an assignment. This meant that I knew of every job opening in my field and had access to a bottomless pool of job opportunities. Whenever I referred people, I immediately called to tell them. I think this earned me a certain amount of respect among friends and colleagues. Over time, friends who were looking for jobs would call me to see if I knew of any relevant searches underway. They would also return the favor and refer search firms to me; further deepening my pool of opportunities and relationships.

Introduction-Based Networking

Although Ron LaLiberte was a headhunter and he did get paid by Prime for finding me, the reason it happened was because he gave me a very strong referral and Paul Ardito (the hiring manager) trusted his opinion. In my experience, this is the best way to shortcut the hiring process and get to the "head of the line" of candidates. It is also one of the best ways to land a job.

A colleague of mine, John Davies, has written a book titled **The $100,000+ Career**: The New Approach to Networking for Executive Job Change. It is a handbook for using Introduction Based Networking to find a new job. If the time has come to search for greener pastures, I recommend you buy his book and put it to work. In lieu of that, here is an interview with John that encapsulates the essence of his technique.

Profile John Davies
A Strategy for When the Pastures Aren't So Green

John Davies is truly a well rounded man. He's traveled the world, started companies, and today he leads the Sustainability Forum at AMR Research in Boston. He has also written one the best career books I've ever read—The $100,000+ Career; The New Approach to Networking for Executive Job Change. John has developed a technique for helping people find a job when they need it most; when they're out of work.

John's father died at an early age and thus he started working when he was quite young. For his entire early career he always had a job and never gave the business of "finding a new one" a second thought. In 1985 he started a software company in southern California that turned out to be quite successful. By 1998, the company had grown to $40 million in annual sales and had turned a profit every quarter. They were well positioned for the kind of IPO (Initial Public Offering) that was creating overnight millionaires throughout Silicon Valley in those days. John and his co-founder decided it was time to bring in "a professional CEO." The two men stepped back and handed the reins of the business over to an outside executive. Unfortunately, the CEO turned out to be a bust. After months of bumping heads, John left the firm and eventually the outside CEO sold the company with little return to the original shareholders.

For the first time in John's life he found himself "on the street" looking for a job. In the process of finding his next job, John discovered the techniques that are revealed in his book. Like most of us, he ran the gamut trying job web sites, executive search firms, and his existing network. Not only was this unsuccessful, but it wasn't much fun. One day it occurred to John that he could ask members of his network for something other than a job; he could ask for an introduction to another contact that might be able to help. Once he reduced the magnitude of his request for assistance, two things happened. First, people started returning his phone calls again; and second, he could play a numbers game and dramatically increase his contact pool; in effect "kiss a lot more frogs." This epiphany was the genesis for his book.

John and I sat down recently on a snowy morning in Boston and he shared a few additional highlights from his unusual approach to working your job search network.

The Second Call Let Down
"Even a casual acquaintance will take your first call when you're starting your job search campaign. They'll talk a good game and maybe even ask around to see if there are any openings. But when you call back a week later to follow-up and they've got nothing for you, the tone of the conversation takes a change for the worse. You're getting depressed because you're not finding a job and so are they since they can't help you. If you just keep asking the same question, pretty soon they'll stop taking your calls just to avoid the pain."

It's Not Who You Know, It's Who They Know
"Let's face it, if you had a great personal network full of people who could give you your next job, you won't be unemployed. You would have simply made a few calls when things got bad and landed your next gig before your last paycheck cleared. Don't just keep burning bridges badgering people to hire you when they can't, ask them to do something they can do; ask them to give you an introduction to someone new. Not only is it a lot easier on them, they're likely to give you multiple introductions. And in time the people they introduce you to can also make multiple introductions. That's how you turn your job search into a numbers game. Get a hundred introductions and you will find a new job."

You're Only On Their Radar as Long as You're on the Phone
"You might think the people in your network are worrying about your job search day and night, but they aren't. The truth is as soon as they hang up the

phone, you're forgotten. This means you need to work them while you have them on the phone. Get the names of people they can introduce you to, contact information, and, most importantly, a time frame for making the introduction. If you do that you'll have a fair chance of getting something useful out of them. If you let them hang up with a promise to think about it, forget it."

Create a Conspiracy

"Most people want to help you from the bottom of their hearts, but they also want to stay away from lost causes. Make it fun for them to help you, "keep score" on the number of introductions you've made, tell them who you're talking to, and especially tell them about successful opportunities they've helped you uncover. Make them co-conspirators in your search."

The Better Your Relationship, The Better the Introduction

"A lot of people think the best network is one full of company presidents, CEO's, and board members. Don't get me wrong, those are great people to know, but they better really know you pretty well if they're going to do you any good. High ranking executives are busy people and don't waste time with casual acquaintances. When it comes to scoring introductions, I'll take a neighbor, relative, or former coworker who has known me well for a long period of time over some executive vice president who couldn't pick me out of a crowd any day. People who know you well can speak passionately about your strengths and they're the ones who are most motivated to help. Face it, if you really had a good relationship with any of those top executives in your network, you wouldn't be out on the street looking for a job."

Catch A Rising Star

Developing a pool of headhunters or leaning on colleagues for introductions are great techniques for finding a new opportunity, but they don't compare with following someone you know—a rising star—into a new company.

Getting a new job this way bears little similarity to the other techniques listed above. The interview process is pure joy. You don't have to sell yourself; you're both simply "assessing the fit." If you're hired, you're immediately in the middle of the action and you just get deeper with each successive day. Most importantly, you have an incredible sense of job security because you know that as long as the star you're attached to continues to shine and you do your job, you'll always be employed.

Unfortunately, picking a true star that will shine on for decades is not as easy as it sounds. First, you have to start the process long before you start thinking about a new job. Also, people in high places are not always rising stars; they may be slowly falling, or not necessarily the people of deep integrity or loyalty you thought they were. Recognizing a fast moving peer as a potential long term star is also a crap shoot. They may be moving fast because they're stepping on people along the way, they're heavily into politics, or they're simply cutting corners. People like this can drag you down as easily as they can help you along. Way back in Strategy Three: Your New Job I talked about "befriending with caution" when you're starting a new position and offered a rough template for the kind of people you should associate with when you enter a new job. This template also serves as a screen to separate true rising stars from imposters. Essentially there are five character traits to look out for when selecting a rising star (see Strategy Three for details).

1. **Well Connected**

2. **On The Move**

3. **Apolitical**

4. **Experienced**

5. **Broadly Appreciated**

Of course, this will only tell you if they are a rising star, not necessarily your rising star. In order for someone with all these traits to be your rising star, they must also believe in you. You must bring something to their team that they value deeply. If you find this person and have this kind of relationship, you will never have to worry about locating new job opportunities.

Surviving The Resignation Ordeal

Regardless of how you find your next job, sooner or later you'll have to "pull the trigger": accept the offer, tender your resignation, and transition over. Everyone thinks this is a wonderful time, but they're wrong. As I said earlier, it's more like a six-month root canal. You'll endure many sleepless nights as you ponder what to do. If you're married, you'll want your spouse's input, which may actually make your decision more difficult. Your spouse may be afraid of the risk and pressure you to stay put. Or they may trivialize the significance of the decision and pressure you to take a chance even though you're not so sure. Then once you finally submit your resignation, all those other people you've been living with at work for 50 hours a week will start casting doubt on your decision.

There are few things you can do to help you through this. First, make sure you've gone through the three-step process described earlier to convince yourself this is the right thing to do. Second, take a piece of paper and start keeping a t-chart detailing all of your major concerns and benefits of making the move as well as the pros and cons associated with each of them. You should list everything, including things that involve your family. This should be a working document; every time you think of something add it to the list. Study every "con" and try to think of ways to mitigate the downside risk. Play devil's advocate with every "pro" and convince yourself that it's legitimate.

Before you pull the trigger and drop off your resignation, do one more thing. Think about what it would take for you to change your mind and stay. If it's a trivial list and all that your boss needs to do is make a minor concession, perhaps you should reconsider. But if the list of things it would take to make you stay is beyond a reasonable expectation of reality, you're probably doing the right thing. Making the list will prepare you in the event your boss asks you, "What will it take to change your mind?" No matter how well you prepare for this meeting, it's going to be as much fun as dumping someone you've been dating for months.

The final stage of the painful process comes when you start work at your new job. Your inability to contribute at first will make you uneasy and even bored at times. You may find yourself daydreaming about your old job and start second guessing your decision. This is very natural and very difficult to ignore. Go back and review Strategy Three: Your New Job for a tactical handbook on how to survive and thrive in your first six months.

Desperate Measures

Like many of the lessons in Career Secret Sauce, there are certain pitfalls to changing jobs that should be avoided for your sanity and well-being.

Leaving the Door Open to Change Your Mind: More often than not, your current boss's first reaction will be to convince you to stay. Losing employees is viewed as a managerial weakness and no one wants that black mark on their record. Also, there is a certain "badge of honor" that goes to a manager who is able to turn someone around. If they ask and you leave the door open—even a crack—you will be subjecting yourself to even more anguish. Also, know that if you do acquiesce and stay, you're position is likely to be marginalized in the future. You will never be fully trusted again, new responsibilities will be given to others, and over time you may find yourself becoming expendable. That's why you have to be sure you're doing the right thing before you resign.

Double Dipping: I'm sure for many of you this may sound like a nutty idea, but it happens more often than you think. In today's workplace, where more and more

193

employers are offering work at home flexibility, it is becoming possible for people to start a new job while still collecting a paycheck from their old employer. I have seen it happen multiple times in the last decade. Usually, it's just for a limited period of time. Someone accepts the new job without resigning from the old one. They continue to "work at home" at their old job after they start their new job through the wonders of email, Blackberries, and cell phones. Then after a week or two on the new job they eventually resign, give two weeks' notice and effectively double dip for over a month. I have also seen the case where a remote salesman who had no physical office actually attempted to do this for an extended period of time, working for a competitor no less. Eventually he was caught and when the original employer contacted the competitor to confirm the deceit, he ended up being fired from both jobs.

You Can Never Go Back: There are a few recurring dreams (nightmares) that multiple people report having. The most common are flying, falling, standing in a room full of people naked, or being back in school taking a test that you never studied for. I have had all of these. There is another one that comes back to me even today and that's the dream where I've gone back to work for a company I left years ago. At first it's fun, then I start to worry about my current job and eventually I remember all the reasons why I left the old place and wake up in a cold sweat. Perhaps this sounds farfetched, but I can tell you from reading thousands of résumés that this happens more often than you think. People take a new job, don't like it, and six months to a year later call up their old boss and go back. It may feel like the right thing to do, but it is the professional equivalent of moving back home to live in your parent's basement. A double tenure on your résumé will speak volumes about your inner make up. Sure it's possible to make a bad move and find yourself in a new job you hate, but returning to you old job, rather than finding another just looks weak. If you're thinking about making this move, consider it your last career change. You will most likely end up staying with your old employer for life.

The Necessary Evil

Searching for greener pastures is never easy. If it feels easy, you may be making a mistake. Make sure when you start your career that you build up your network, help headhunters, and keep a sharp eye out for rising stars, even if looking for a new job is the furthest thing from your mind. Ask yourself on a regular basis if it's time to go. Once you're convinced it is, take it slow, cover all the bases and make sure you find the best new job possible.

Good Luck!

THE FINAL STRATEGY

Just Do the Right Thing

I hope *Career Secret Sauce* has given you everything you need to know to start a great career. A lot of these lessons have been based on insider tricks, while others are almost common sense. It is not my intent to suggest that you trick anyone into helping you to have a great career; I'm just asking you to do the right thing.

Invest all the time you can getting your career off to a solid start before all of the other realities of life come crashing down. Use internships to achieve the goal of having the job offer you want in hand before graduation.

Nurturing a great reputation, using your time wisely, and developing the communication skills needed to master the art of presentation is not trickery. This is exactly what your boss and everyone around you wants you to do; it's simply the right thing to do.

Don't rush your promotions, learn the art of Promotionology. If you make a mistake and need to pull off a saving move, face it head on and deal with it. It's your mess; you clean it up!

Finally, treat each employer with respect and savor every job as if it were a fine wine. But know that the time will come when you just have to move on. Take it very seriously and you will always end up doing the right thing.

What happens if everyone buys this book and follows the nine strategies of Career Secret Sauce?

I think the world would be a better place.

About The Author

The best lessons are often the ones that are learned the hard way; through blood, sweat and tears. Dave Horne has had plenty of them, both good and bad.

Dave Horne's career expertise comes directly from the action on the front lines of corporate America. Like many fast track young executives, his early drive for success almost destroyed his career. Facing the prospect of being fired for the second time, he met his greatest career test. He scrambled to keep a paycheck by accepting a demotion. Licking his wounds, he made a pledge to never let it happen again.

Dave Horne began researching career success in the trenches. He carefully studied the behavior of people who seemed to cruise along; those who enjoyed regular promotion, job security and still had plenty of free time. More importantly, Dave also studied the mistakes of those who had crashed and burned like himself. It didn't take long to discover that career happiness had little to do with job advancement.

Learning from his own mistakes and applying what he had learned, Dave jumped from decades of middle management to corporate vice president in a few short years; he enjoyed a steady flow of new job offers and most importantly, found that his job security allowed him to spend more time with his family.

Dave has been refining his formula for career success known as "Career Secret Sauce" for over a decade, used it to teach others how to achieve the coveted goal of a balanced career, and now reveals it in this book.

Dave left his career in general management in 2005 to write Career Secret Sauce; 9 Winning Strategies for Building a Great Career.

Although his formula for success applies to everyone, his passion is to help young people avoid painful mistakes and excel from college through the first ten years of their career.

Dave Horne holds a Bachelor of Science degree from the University of Massachusetts and an MBA in Strategic Planning from Northeastern University in Boston.